W9-AVL-791

# THE COMPLETE BOOK OF FUND-RAISING WRITING

## DON FEY

© 1995 by Don Fey.

All rights reserved under Pan-American Copyright Conventions. Published in
the United States by The Morris-Lee Publishing Group, Rosemont, New Jersey.
Unauthorized reproduction of this book is forbidden by law.

International Standard Book Number (ISBN): 0-9645356-0-2
Library of Congress Catalog Card Number: 95-76071

The Morris-Lee
Publishing Group

P.O. Box 218, Rosemont, New Jersey 08556

## Dedication

This book is dedicated to all the fund raisers, writers, and volunteers who have stared at the ceiling at four o'clock in the morning wondering why they ever took the job in the first place.

" ...the sole carriers of information are words; and these, as everybody knows, are hard to handle."

Jacques Barzun
*The Modern Researcher*

# Preface

In communications, good writing, like good pitching, can be ninety percent of the game. From my work at fund-raising seminars and conferences, I know there are many persons who want or could use help with their writing assignments, many others whose futures depend on a fund-raising writer's success or failure, and many donors who would appreciate simpler, clearer requests. This book is designed for use by busy people who need to get a writing job done *now*.

- If you are a veteran writer, it will help you do a better job.
- If you are a fund-raising administrator, it will show you what to look for in hiring a writer and how to review the finished product.
- If you are a beginning writer, it will give you confidence.

Writing good fund-raising copy is a full-time job. It takes toughness, imagination, and creativity. You've got to work at it, but it's worth it. Improving your writing skills will make you more valuable to the organization and put you in touch with people at the top. What's more, you will more often find yourself involved with development projects from beginning to end. That's a reward few jobs offer at any level. How far you can go with better writing skills is up to you, but it's no secret that many top executives today have strong communications backgrounds.

There's a use for fund-raising writing skills at all levels of development, whether you're the literary type or like to do administrative work. In addition to straight editorial work, other development jobs that bank heavily on good writing skills, for example, include major gifts coordinator, corporate and foundation relations officer, prospect researcher, and stewardship writer.

Career writing possibilities in fund raising include a range of opportunities in such diverse fields as science, medicine, education, the arts, social service, public radio and TV, recreation, and religion. And the work is rewarding. In addition to making an excellent living, I have had the pleasure of helping to provide schools with new professorships and scholarships, to advance medical and biological research, to build new teaching centers for business, science, and the fine arts, to establish community arts programs, to strengthen volunteer programs, and to set up learning and recreational facilities for mentally and physically challenged children.

This book reflects ideas, skills, and techniques I picked up over more than 25 years of writing news stories, proposals, brochures, speeches, scripts, case statements, magazine articles, press releases, and ad copy. Some methods I worked out on my own, others came from working with other editors and writers and reading their work, and still others from attending or teaching seminars and workshops.

For what it's worth, in this book I invite you to share what I have learned about the business of fund-raising writing. But be forewarned. There are no reproductions for you to copy. Only guidelines for you to follow and lessons to learn. You will have to think. One reason I have not included actual full-length samples of development writing is that they would make the book far too big and expensive. And they would soon seem out-of-date.

Another reason is that many persons would be tempted to just copy the samples. I don't want you to copy anything. I want you to understand. At the end of each chapter are exercises you can do and tips on where you can easily obtain current examples to work with. But even if you don't have time to do the exercises or get the samples, this handbook will see you through virtually every fund-raising writing task. It is all you will really need to do a better job. As you will see, fund-raising writing is a fine way to earn a living and help change our world for the better.

Who could ask for more?

Don Fey
Drexel Hill, Pennsylvania
December 1994

# Acknowledgements

I wish to thank the following persons and organizations for helping to make this book possible. First of all, my wife, Jeanne, who made it possible for me to have the time to do the work and who gave me all the encouragement and support I needed.

Next, my thanks to James Morris-Lee, who helped me get from the idea stage to the writing stage and beyond. My thanks, too, to everyone in The Morris-Lee Publishing Group for their contributions: to Steve Smith for his graphic design and production work and to Mary Kane and Jennifer Ellsworth for their administrative and technical support.

I also wish to thank two outstanding fund-raising professionals, Kathleen M. Watson and M. Jane Williams for their comments and thoughts. My thanks also to Kay Mills at Thomas Jefferson University for her insights into special events and to Frank McGovern and the rest of the Development Office staff there for their assistance and cooperation.

Finally, I must thank my former colleagues at the University of Pennsylvania at whose literary knees I first came to appreciate the subtleties and challenges of fund-raising writing: Shirley Winters, Wayne Barr, and the late J. Crosier Schaefer, a master of the game.

# Contents

# PART ONE

# The World of Fund Raising Today

# Chapter One

# American Philanthropy: Satisfying A Public Need

**B**EFORE anyone can be an effective fund-raising writer, he or she needs to grasp the nature and scope of America's penchant for giving. Fund raising is only indirectly related to money. The spirit behind all ethical development work has to do with what Eric Hoffer, the late philosopher-longshoreman, once called "things which are not." Fund raisers are futurists selling ideas, opportunities, prestige, and even immortality of a sort. And the buyers are persons from every walk of life, some rich, but many not.

When Bruce M. Brown, then administrator of The W.W. Smith Charitable Trusts, told a Philadelphia audience of more than 400 fund raisers, "You and I are in the vision business," he summed up the moving force behind all successful fund raising. Nonprofit agencies give the public a means for social expression, a chance to make a difference. Donors need to hitch their wagon to a star, even if it is somebody else's star. They need to help visions become realities. *Why* they do it is not the writer's concern and never should be. Charitable giving is an emotionally charged, highly personal act. Big donors will rarely be able to tell you exactly why they decided to support one request over another. Nor can corporate or foundation giving officers do much better. "Grantmakers are not endowed with infinite wisdom which descends to them from the heavens," said Brown.

In other words, donors need help in making decisions. It's tough work giving money away, and since most people don't know why they give to one cause and not another, it's up to us, as writers, to give them as many reasons, ideas, and opportunities to choose our cause as we can. If there is a common denominator in successful appeals, it is this: They always, always, focus on securing the well being of living things—human, animal, and ecological. Remember this one fact and your letters and proposals will home in on the well-spring of caring running deep in us all.

As the philosopher, Blaise Pascal, wrote, "The heart hath its reasons which reason knoweth not."

## Where the money comes from

No other nation even comes close to the United States in charitable giving. Individually and collectively Americans love to give money away. Why else would we part with billions of dollars a year to benefit churches, colleges, medical research, arts groups, and other popular causes?

About eighty percent of these billions comes from private citizens, including wealthy individuals. Foundations, which by law have to give away at least six percent of their endowment every year, account for another fifteen percent (and just ten East Coast foundations account for most of this). Corporations, which keep one eye on the stockholders and the other on the competition, rarely give away their annual tax-deductible maximum of two percent of gross earnings, but they still make up the last five percent of all charitable gifts. Their gifts are usually business-related and based on how the company is doing and what looks best for them in the long run. But give they do, millions upon millions of dollars every year.

## A vital part of the economy

You don't have to be Milton Friedman or John Maynard Keynes to see that nonprofits have become the vital "third leg" on the American economic stool. The other two being, of course, corporate and government spending. I say "vital" because the nonprofit sector is the prime source of new ideas and new ventures which fuel our vision as a people. Nowhere is the revolutionary nature of the American psyche more apparent than in the third sector of the economy. And private gifts are the fastest way to beat the built-in roadblocks and red tape of our overloaded state and federal grants systems. Even though corporate and foundation gifts do have to make it past screening committees, peer review groups, and hawkeyed accountants, appeals get through the private giving process a lot faster than they do with the government.

Private gifts are the catalyst that makes things happen now, when they will do the most good, and not at some dim point in the future. They bring freedom to the intellectual marketplace and let ideas flourish that wouldn't have a chance with federal agencies. Every year charitable giving spurs teaching and research, strengthens health care, sponsors art and cultural events, and nourishes private social agencies that ease the burden on tax-paying wage-earners. I have seen multimillion-dollar personal gifts for professorships, laboratories, buildings, scholarships, research, and fine arts and cultural programs take place in a matter of weeks.

In some cases, the key element was a well-written, two- or three-page "conversation memo" laying out a rough picture of the opportunity and the action plan. I can say, too, that many of the new ideas, products, and services which make the United States such a dynamic, flexible society would never have existed without the seed money for basic research provided by private support.

Fund raising is the "profit margin" that keeps nonprofit agencies in business today and lets them plan for tomorrow. Nonprofit agencies, furthermore, pump up the economy through the jobs they create and the people they employ. There are currently 350,000 tax-free, IRS-certified, nonprofit organizations in this country and some of the larger ones employ 5,000 people or more. According to the book, *Fund Raising as a Profession*, by Dr. Robert F. Carbone of the University of Maryland, about two-thirds of all professional fund-raisers work at educational or medical institutions. The other third work for social service organizations and arts and cultural groups. In some areas, the nonprofit university or medical center *is* the fund-raising community.

## Fund-raising writing as part of a larger strategy

No fund-raising appeal can be better than what goes into it, and this information will only be as good as the people doing an organization's planning. Although the writer has much to say about what a fund-raising letter, proposal, or publication will look and sound like, what finally goes into these items results from:

1. Trustees and directors making policy and setting organizational goals,
2. Management working with line staff to find out what's needed and how to get it, and
3. The development staff, whether it's one person or many, trying

to match donors with projects and design a solid fund-raising platform.

Each of these groups has its own agenda and priorities which must somehow be saluted, shaped, and presented to the outside world as a cohesive, well-thought-out fund-raising program that will benefit the entire operation, the local community, and even, on occasion, the nation or the world.

In a small organization, many of the executive decisions needed to sort out all this planning rest with a single person—an all-purpose development officer/researcher/writer. Even in larger operations, which might include a major gifts officer, an annual giving officer, a planned giving and bequests expert, researchers, stewardship people, and secretaries, it will often be left up to the writer to divine what the organization's message is and figure out how to get it across. In this sense, fund-raising writers wield a certain amount of power in influencing executive thinking. Conversely, they also catch a lot of heat when things go wrong. Happy and rare is the writer free of political conflict and whose directions from on high come through in a loud, clear, and singular voice.

## A fundamentally different product

"Well," you say, "all that sounds great, but it still doesn't tell us what makes fund-raising writing different from other kinds of team-based writing such as a movie or TV script, a magazine ad, or a speech for a major politician."

The difference is this: The fund-raising document must nearly always stand alone, and nine times out of ten, all the money is riding on it. There are no unique effects or electronic augmentation to punch it up, no special positioning or dynamic art work to separate it from the competition, no gifted orator to breath new life into your words. All the reader has to go on is what you said and how you said it. And relying on that may be a new community theater, a violence-prevention program for elementary-school children, or a cure for multiple sclerosis. And that's not to mention the development office's budget, your reputation, and all the jobs, goods, and services attendant on the success of what you have written.

## The scope of fund-raising writing

A piece of copy calling for the distinctive touch of the fund-raising writer can range from something as sensitive and complex as a case statement to a simple, but highly important thank-you note. Other

6

documents that fall somewhere within this range are prospectuses, mission statements, proposals, brochures, newsletters, speeches, scripts, plaque and citation copy, direct-mail appeals, gift recognition books, magazine stories and advertisements, newspaper columns, position papers, stewardship and research reports, and informational letters and conversation memos.

A fund-raising writer should not only be capable of handling these assignments but should expect to do so in any development operation that is covering all the bases in the way it is supposed to do. While each of these assignments has a specific use and purpose in fulfilling the organization's fund-raising mission, they share the common principle of informing potential donors about the organization and inspiring them to support it. Here is a brief overview of what each of these particular tools should accomplish:

### Case statements and prospectuses
Key items in any major campaign, these documents outline the organization's mission, its vision and plans for the future, and which areas are most worthy of support. The main difference between a case statement and a prospectus is that a case statement will affix a "price" to various components of a fund-raising program, but a prospectus stops short of that.

### Mission Statements
These, like people, come in all shapes and sizes. When done right, they serve as an excellent guide for drawing up the case statement or setting up a proposal.

### Brochures
Used to back up a proposal or mailing with some kind of visual impact; useful when they support a specific purpose, but not as all-around effective as some people think. (Development officers tend to like them because they lend an illusion of progress and accomplishment.)

### Newsletters
Great for making new friends and keeping old ones if they are well-designed and well-written. They keep you in touch with donors and let you acknowledge them directly by printing their names and pictures. They let you tell more of your story. And the friendlier and newsier the better. If people have sent you money they are usually interested in receiving a newsletter about what their gifts are doing. They will almost always read a newsletter and will rarely toss it away without looking it over first. Newsletters are also generally much more effective and appeal-

ing to your readers than a brochure. A brochure says "read me sometime." A newsletter says "read me now." Newsletters are cheap, too. You can print them on anything from a mimeo to a copying machine, if need be.

### Direct-Mail Appeals

The bread-and-butter tool for small nonprofits. A good cause, a good list, and a good letter can work wonders. Direct mail also lays the groundwork for larger requests from major prospects in the future.

### Gift Recognition Books

These come and go in favor, but if done in a simple, tasteful fashion, they offer a nice way to salute your friends, let them know the company they're keeping, and slip in a few casual plugs for the cause. Always use good new pictures and captions that tell your story for the year. Avoid "firing squad" line-ups or "grip-and-grin" art.

### Position Papers, Informational Letters, Conversation Memorandums

These serve a number of purposes, sometimes internal, sometimes external. They come before making an actual request and help to get everyone on the same wavelength for subsequent meetings.

### Stewardship Reports and Letters

It's important to thank donors early and often. A letter should be tailored to the size of the gift and its overall importance to the organization. A report is usually made once a year to the big-hitter donors who have made extraordinary gifts in the past (and will probably do so in the future). The challenge is making these reports different and interesting year after year.

### Newspaper Columns, Magazine Stories, and Advertisements

As you might guess, these are written mainly for house organs such as alumni publications, but they are also good for raising visibility of the development function. Mostly, they focus on the happy results of successful drives or help to lay the groundwork for a new one.

### Scripts

Whether it's a new audio cassette for visitors, the annual dinner dance speech for the President's Club, or a talk in front of local business people, a script can avoid mistakes, keep the agony to a minimum, and make the boss look good. On a good day, you might even get your message across.

Here are a few sequences illustrating how these various forms of fund-raising writing relate to each other in the fund-raising process:

1. A letter of inquiry is sent to a foundation or corporation to feel them out. This is followed by a position paper to be used at a meeting of foundation officers and representatives of the non-profit organization. Things go well, and a proposal is submitted for consideration. The grant request is funded and immediately thank-you letters are sent. Later, stewardship reports will be submitted as required or appropriate. The gift may also be acknowledged in a gift book or with the dedication of a plaque or the awarding of citations for exceptional efforts.

2. A telethon call is followed by a direct-mail appeal with a pledge card. A follow-up brochure is mailed and the gift comes in. A gift receipt and thank-you note are sent. Later the donor is listed in the newsletter for all givers, and, if the gift merits it, in the gift book or annual report.

## Exercises

- Become familiar with your local library's reference resources for fund-raising research and guidance.
- Read Harold J. Seymour's *Designs for Fund Raising* (Fund Raising Institute).
- Read several recent copies of *The Chronicle of Philanthropy* at your local college or university library.
- Write to the National Society of Fund Raising Executives (NSFRE) and the Council for the Advancement and Support of Education (CASE) for recent articles on career opportunities in fund raising and reports on current salaries in the field. They do these annually.
- Find the name and address of your local NSFRE chapter. Call and ask for their newsletter and membership requirements.
- Get a membership list of local nonprofits from your local NSFRE chapter. Get a job interview with one or two of them as a potential freelancer. Find out what they pay.
- Call a foundation executive and ask for an informational interview about their mission, including the scope of grants and gifts.

# Chapter Two

# What's So Different About Fund-Raising Writers?

**N**ow that you have some idea about the philosophical and economic impact of fund-raising writing and the scope of writing needs, you can see what good writing means to a development program. But there are still many unanswered questions. For instance, if you are an administrator, you'll probably want to know which characteristics and credentials a "fund-raising" writer should have. You'd also probably like to find out whatever it is that fund-raising writers seem to know that other writers don't. In a word, "What are their qualifications?" And "How many years of experience, for example, are considered enough, and what kind of experience is the best experience?"

Certainly, these are two major concerns. Sometimes breadth of experience will be more significant than the number of years on the job, for fund-raising writing is nothing if not diverse. Some writers fairly new to the game, however, seem to know instinctively what chords to strike and what notes to play with a minimum of advice.

## Key characteristics of a fund-raising writer

What I look for, when hiring a new writer, is the ability to write interesting, *imaginative* copy. The trouble with most fund-raising copy is that you can substitute one nonprofit group's name for another in a piece (provided they are in the same line of work), and it won't make any difference. I also like to see samples of any creative work an applicant may have done. It could be something written for class or a piece submitted to a magazine. I tend to lean toward people who also have computer skills and a flair for design. In established writers, I look for diversity of experience in addition to the ability to write clean, tight copy.

Some writers, by the way, resist learning new tricks such as computer-based writing, layout, and design. In a small shop or a large one, one writer with a computer and a printer can cover a lot of bases. A list of qualifications for hiring a new writer would include the following:

- A degree in journalism or English. (Advanced degrees in science, business, engineering, etc., are useful if they apply to the organization's purpose.)
- Reporting, advertising, marketing, or public relations experience of one to three years.
- A gift for writing punchy, interesting copy.
- Proof that he or she can meet a deadline.
- Computer skills.
- A well-read, curious person with a broad range of interests.
- Compatibility with other staff members and the the ability to take direction, work independently, and hold up under editing and criticism. In addition, a thick skin and a sense of humor are definitely a plus.

These same basic requirements also hold true for hiring senior staff writers except that they should have a proven track record in writing case statements, proposals, and direct-mail appeals for one or more nonprofit agencies. They should also know a great deal about the role of other development operations including major prospect solicitation, prospect research, stewardship, corporate and foundation relations, and so on. These days an experienced writer will know what is and isn't selling in the philanthropic world.

## Filling the bill

Those who seem to do best at fund-raising writing are generally well-read and appreciate writing in all its forms including fiction, drama, poetry, and the classic forms of the essay. In fact, of all writing skills, a gift for the essay is probably the most valuable to fund-raising writers, because many types of assignments deal with a single subject.

By "literate" I mean someone who reads 25 to 50 books a year on a broad range of subjects. In this light, English majors may seem to have a slight edge over persons with a background in journalism or communications. In fact, what's best is a combination of the two. The insights of the romantic liberal arts intellectual are needed to balance the views of process-minded clients such as engineers, scientists, physicians, accountants, lawyers, and administrators.

Most good reporters and editors will have more than a nodding acquaintance with the classics. They enjoy the added advantage of knowing how to interview and write under pressure. Until recently, few, if any, writers started out by specializing in fund raising, but the rapid growth of the field and the stepped-up demand for persons who can turn information into communication has started to attract beginners. Versatility is important because fund-raising writing is by nature highly structured. There is a format (not a formula) for each type of assignment, and the person who doesn't know how and when to expand on, or digress from, established patterns will soon go stale and start to "burn out."

Burn-out, stemming from the repetitive nature of many development writing assignments, seems to hit more younger fund-raising writers than veterans. However, I continue to get calls from young people who want to be fund-raising writers, asking me for advice on how to break into the field. (There are, in fact, two or three entry-level positions they can seek that make it relatively easy to get started. See "Tips for Newcomers" in Chapter 17.)

## What fund-raising writers will do for you that you can't do for yourself

Few authors on fund-raising subjects manage to get very far without quoting or paraphrasing the late Harold "Sy" Seymour, whose book, *Designs for Fund Raising*, written more than a generation ago is still the bible on fund-raising basics, including how to write copy that gets results. Those most concerned with the success of a proposal or campaign, said Sy, are least qualified to sit down and write about it for public consumption. They're too close to the subject and have too much at stake.

When people ask me why an insider such as an administrator, professor, or trustee can't draft a letter or proposal just as well as I can, I tell them it's for the same reason that General Motors doesn't let the engineers and designers write the ad copy for the latest line of cars: they know how to build them, but they don't know how to sell them. It took a clever ad agency writer to convert technical terms like "rack and pinion steering" and "overhead cams" into buzz words.

The professional fund-raising writer knows what the public, corporate, and foundation hot buttons are and when to press them in pitching a proposal or piece of direct mail. The best writers have a knack for casting their ideas in the best possible light. Writers, moreover, usually have a good grip on things like printing and design costs; ties with affordable, but competent, photographers and designers; a reasonable idea of what a mail house or a list manager can do for a project; and what contemporary trends are in seeking support. They can quickly outline the merits of one type of appeal over another. And, in addition to writing copy that "sings," the writer can keep fund raisers on track regarding the many other elements that go into a major development piece. As Professor Harold Hill's competitors in *The Music Man* liked to say, "Ya gotta know the territory!"

## What fund-raising writers can't do for you

There have been times in the past when I saw $10 million gifts made on a handshake. No more. There were also times when I was called into a meeting and told that "The Warbucks Foundation gave so-and-so a million dollars for their lively arts program. We want to submit a proposal for the same amount for something similar. What do you think?" It only took a few questions to resolve that the only information my client had to offer was that he wanted money. No program existed, none had really been contemplated, and there was no market for one if it did. Sounds stupid, doesn't it? Yet it happens every day. All that was lacking from his project—other than money—was a need, planning, and institutional backing. The idea, if you can call it that, was "Let's see if they'll give us the money and then we'll put something together to fit." Oddly enough, twenty years ago people used to get away with this kind of thing routinely. No more.

No fund-raising writer can sell a bad idea. Nor can he or she make up for a lack of planning and insight, tell you what your organization's policy and practices should be in carrying out its mission, or help you plan and manage your operating budget. These things must come first, and you have to be able to demonstrate to any prospective donor that you have not only done your homework but have done it exceeding well. The worst thing someone seeking funds can do, in fact, is warp his or her organization's purpose to fit someone else's goals merely to keep funding levels high.

# Chapter Three

# Preparing to Sell Your Ideas to Prospects

N today's competitive fund-raising market, it's vital to make your organization stand out from the competition. The people you're interested in asking for support probably don't know you, they don't know your organization, and they don't know what you want them to do. Good communications will help you reach them. Poor communications can lose them forever.

Here's a story that illustrates this principle:

Two fellows were out hiking in backwoods Alaska. Suddenly they found themselves face-to-face with an 8-foot, 2,000-pound Kodiak bear. The first hiker sat down, got his running shoes out of his backpack, and started to change over from his hiking boots. "Are you crazy?" said the second hiker, "You can't outrun that bear."

"I don't have to outrun him," said the first hiker, "I only have to outrun you."

That's pretty much the way it is in fund-raising communications. You only have to outrun the nearest competitor.

Not all foundations are alike; neither are corporations. And individuals are the most unpredictable of all. The wealthiest friend of your organization can lead you a merry chase for years, promising everything and delivering nothing, even in the will. And if he or she does leave you a bundle, spouses, children, and relatives can hold up the payoff for years.

If individuals can change their nature and their minds as they age, so can foundations and corporations as circumstances change in their world and the world around them. A new executive director for a major foundation, for example, can mean a total about-face for that organization in its policy; a foundation that routinely supported health and social causes is suddenly only interested in arts and cultural affairs. Writers and organizations have to learn to go with the flow in these instances and gird themselves against the need to take new tacks or sail hard against the wind.

## Who gets to play

Many foundations will only deal with "blue chip" nonprofit organizations, those that they have been funding for decades. Proposals from newcomers or small community groups rarely make the final funding cut. Is this fair? No. Is this good policy? No. But it's safe. A foundation or corporate funding officer knows he is on safe ground approving appeals from "big hitters," even though these grants may prove to be less fruitful in the end than a more innovative, adventurous proposal. It's their game, so they have final say as to who gets to play. Other foundations will only do business with the "neighborhood" crowd. Out-of-towners need not apply. In some cases, this is the way the foundation was set up by the founder, in others, it's just easier to keep the giving program down to manageable size. Corporations, especially, tend to give more and larger gifts closer to home, or at least in those areas where they actually have offices, plants, or do other kinds of business. "Enlightened self-interest" is the operating principal. Most of these practices are coming under more and more criticism in the press.

Individuals are even harder to pin down. Sometimes a big gift can be negotiated and secured in a matter of weeks, but with most big givers the courtship process usually takes years. The reason for this being, of course, the strong possibility that more than one major gift will be made over the lifetime of the relationship, and there is always the prospect of a substantial bequest. No matter how maddening it can get, we need to stay on the good side of all our prospects.

## Stick to your guns

Patience and forbearance are the order of the day when dealing with the unusually demanding prospect. You want to get your gift with as few strings attached as possible. The worst prospect is one forever dangling promises of large grants that may be made if such-and-so takes place or special terms are met. In writing a proposal, never promise people like this anything for less than the full price and cash on the barrelhead. For example, many schools have gone ahead and named professorships for donors on the basis of a future bequest or when only ten or twenty percent of the cost is in hand. Years later, they find themselves in the sad position of either being left out of the will or pleading for the remainder of the pledge.

Other donors make a game out of getting a facility or a building named for themselves at bargain rates. Do something like this and you're dead as far as future donors are concerned. Once you've established a price, stick to it. The truly committed and informed donor is the one who simply asks how much you need, what for, and where to send the check? Thank heaven a few of them actually still exist.

The fact is, givers give for all kinds of unpredictable reasons: some do it because they have to dispense a certain amount of dollars every year; some do it because they feel guilty about being rich in a world full of misery; some are truly altruistic, kind, and thoughtful; some are glad to be rid of the burden of wealth (Don't laugh, there are many foundations whose sole purpose is the liquidation of principal within a specified period).

No matter what type of prospects you may be dealing with, foundations, corporations, or individuals, they will all need certain things in hand before they can act one way or the other. It's the writer's job to put this information together and put the correct spin on it. A pitch for supporting the fine arts, for instance, should be written and packaged differently for an individual than for a corporation or a foundation.

## Choosing the right approach

Fund raising tools serve a variety of purposes: to inform, inspire, persuade, identify, condition, acknowledge, thank, congratulate, and so on. Heading the list, of course, is to convince the donor that your organization deserves his or her support for this particular project.

There are three basic written tools for telling your story to the people with the money. We'll discuss them all in detail later on, but let's take a look at them as a group before we get down to the nuts and bolts of how they should be written.

- The first, and most common tool, is the **fund-raising proposal**. It is also the most abundant and abused approach. Almost invariably, proposals are too long, too confusing, and too dull. Many get funded in spite of this.

- The second favorite tool is the **letter**. It may be a letter of inquiry seeking to set up a meeting, a proposal in letter form, or a piece of direct mail asking someone to support a special project or the annual fund. Since most of us have written letters, many people tend to think writing a fund-raising letter is not all that different. This is why many organizations' direct-mail appeals fail to produce the desired result. A fund-raising letter is as structured as a sonnet and should be equally memorable and evocative. It is truly an art form of its own and will never entirely lose its use as a fund-raising instrument. Indeed, given the reluctance of most nonprofit executives to make face-to-face personal appeals, direct mail will be with us until electronics completely dominates communications (and the final wall goes up between donors and supplicants).

- The third tool is the **report**. These can be stewardship reports, which are sent periodically to fill a donor in on the grant's progress and maintain a sound relationship for future partnerships, or they can be status reports in the form of white papers which put a prospect in the picture but do not ask directly for financial support. These latter reports, which are sometimes called "conversation memos," serve two purposes. They let the prospect know you're in a business they usually support, and they provide the basis for a future meeting and discussion of mutual aims. Should that happy event transpire, reports are extremely useful for making sure everyone on your side of the table is telling the same story to the prospect and for allowing the prospect to ask pertinent questions without making any immediate commitment.

Less effective, but something which many big nonprofits seem to produce to excess, are expensive, four-color brochures and inexpensive, often poorly thought-out, newsletters. Actually, the money and the emphasis would be better spent if the process were reversed. Brochures date rapidly as names, faces, and fashions change (including graphic design fashions), and they usually lack the "read me now" insistence of a good newsletter.

Newsletters, on the other hand, if they are well-designed and well-written, not only get read thoroughly, but tend to be passed on to others with hand-written comments and suggestions in the margins. You've probably done this in your own office. But how many brochures have you ever done this with? In fact, how often do you read a brochure from cover to cover? With desktop publishing techniques almost universally available and good young designers and journalists in abundance, there is no excuse for the many amateurish newsletters now in circulation.

## A few general guidelines

What, then, is the right tool to use and when? And for what prospect? Are there any general guidelines for informing your decision? Well, let's think about it for a moment. First of all, there are just too many people and too many groups seeking support and too few funding agencies to meet their needs for you to make the wrong decision. In Philadelphia alone, there are some 8,000 supplicant organizations for about 600 area foundations and grant-making corporations, a ratio of about 13 to 1. The true ratio, that of the total number of grantseekers interested in any particular agency, including out-of-town fundseekers, is probably a much bigger number. This is yet another reason only 5 of every 100 proposals get funded. I suspect that gap has been getting bigger in recent times, but the data aren't in yet.

Here's how to save yourself a great deal of grief and fruitless work:

- **After you find out which foundations and corporations are most likely to be interested in your work, phone and get the name of the person now handling grant requests** (they change fast). Sit down and draft him or her a one- or two-page letter of inquiry that tells who you are and what you want. Then follow the letter up with a phone call asking for a meeting (best case) or some guidance on preparing your proposal. Work your way down the whole list until you find someone not only willing to read your proposal, but anxious to see it and discuss it with you. When you are working with a contact on the scene, the odds in favor of receiving a grant rise dramatically. Whether the proposal is a full-length piece of 15 to 20 pages plus appendixes or the shorter, single-spaced "letter proposal" its form will depend on the requirements of the foundation or corporation. If your appeal is to an individual, keep it short, simple, and to the point. No more than five or six double-spaced pages and a one-page budget will do nicely.
- **If your operation can be funded, or is funded, mainly by large numbers of individual contributions, the letter is the route for you to go.** And make it as warm and personal as you can. Proposals, when you submit them, should follow the guidelines above and be project-oriented. Give them something they can sink their teeth into, something with taste, touch, and feel to it. (A reviewer should be able to say, "You know what I like

about this proposal?") Direct-mail appeals sent to a "blind" list usually score successfully with only one to two percent of recipients. When the list is home-grown, however, as in the case of an alumni appeal or a community mailing, the number of successful letters can soar to the 25 or 50 percent level.

- **Reports are sound policy, but they take time and money**. How many you write each year and how detailed they are depend largely on the size of your staff and the time you have at your disposal. When you actually get a grant, an annual or semi-annual accounting of what's being accomplished always sits well with the granting party. If you do most of your work by mail, an annual report letter can set the stage for the next ask. They can even be part of the same mailing. Annual reports for external distribution should always include a page or two, with photos, about recent fund-raising accomplishments and goals. In larger organizations, the development department should always distribute an internal annual report to keep officers and trustees informed of progress and results.

## Exercises

- Get copies of annual reports from your largest local foundations. See what their goals are and what causes they have been funding recently.
- Using the reports, make a list of how many small nonprofits got grants and what the money was for.
- Write for, or get copies of, the annual reports of the Ford, Rockefeller, and Pew Foundations. Repeat the previous two exercises. Are any local groups included in their grants list? Try to get a copy of their successful proposals to study.
- Ask two or three of the biggest local foundations and corporations for their grants guidelines. You'll need the name and address of the person in charge of corporate giving at the latter.
- Think about how you could use letters, reports, or other nonproposal tools in getting a nonprofit's foot in the door with one of the corporations and foundations you have contacted.
- Assemble the material and information you have collected from these first three exercises into your own private reference library.

# PART Two:

# Tools You Will Need

# Chapter Four

# Writing A Solid Proposal

**W**HEN people think of fund-raising writing they usually have proposals in mind. In actual practice, a busy fund-raising writer may only spend half his or her time on proposals. Appeal letters, speeches, plans, citations and resolutions, brochure copy, magazine articles, audiovisual scripts, ad copy, annual reports, stewardship letters, and position papers are just some of the other things that will more than fill up the other hours in the staff writer's week. Still, proposals are the heavy-duty, industrial-strength documents most agencies and nonprofit organizations depend on to raise really big numbers for key projects and programs. For a bigger organization, we could be talking in the $10- to $20-million range; for smaller groups, $5,000 or $10,000 may put their plans on track. Yet, in either case, the proposal's writing and design must be "bullet proof" to have any chance of succeeding. That's why nothing should be left to chance. That's why a proposal should always represent your organization's top priority at this stage in its development or mission. If you have researched and planned well, *a proposal represents your best shot at your best prospect.*

## Why proposals fail

Only about five percent of all proposals ever get funded. The other ninety-five percent go down the tube, even though many persons may have invested long hours in their preparation and submittal. Even a good proposal can be "declined," but most of the losers deserve just what they get. Nothing. Sometimes these proposals fail because not enough work went into researching the prospect and tailoring it to the donor's interest. Sometimes it's because the main idea is buried under a ton of supporting, but useless, detail. Sometimes it's because key elements were missing or weakly stated. As I mentioned earlier, just presenting the information isn't enough, it's how you present it (more and more donors want to hear directly from your experts themselves before considering a proposal) and who you present it to. Either way, the fund-raising writer should always play a role in any document drafted.

## Getting off on the right foot

As you start to prepare your document, keep in mind that most of the time it's not what you're selling, but what the prospect is buying. Before you put a word on paper, you'd better be absolutely certain that you've got the "the right church and the right pew." Once you do begin to write, strive to convey that you're writing about people and their hopes and needs, not an impersonal bureaucratic machine. Proposals appeal to the emotions as much as the intellect. With individual prospects, proposals should evoke such feelings as "Gosh, I've got to help out with this," or "I've been so lucky, let me share my good fortune this way," or "Gee, I'm really proud of them and what they are doing."

The following tips will help you get off on the right foot:

**Be interesting right away.**
Don't let the reaction to your first sentence or paragraph be "So what?" At the heart of every project is a dramatic concept that bears directly on human happiness. Find it and write about it.

**Focus on people and ideas, not money.**
The people who are doing the work and the people who will benefit from it are infinitely more interesting than mounds of statistics or technical procedures. Illuminate some of the faces in the crowd.

**Use simple language.**
"Once upon a time there were three bears." Well, you know the rest. To keep your basic points easy to grasp and retain, simplicity is best.

**Restate and summarize.**
If you need to use scientific, technical, medical, or bureaucratic

material in your proposal, please work with the experts to translate it into a reasonable approximation a lay person can grasp. By the same token, if you have related a long or complex series of steps or events, pause every now and then to sum up for the reader what's just been covered. This will set up the transition into the next segment of the document. For instance, "We have shown the serious nature of the widget shortage, and discussed how we intend to resolve the raw materials crisis at the root of the shortage. We will now outline our plan for restructuring industrial alignments in the communities most affected."

### Work from a good design.

Organize your material before you sit down to write. Arrange your key points in a logical sequence and break each down into its main components. This will keep you from wandering off into internal administrative or procedural fringe areas which may seem terribly important to people on your project team, but hold no real interest for the prospect. Be tough about this.

### Stress the goal, not the method of attaining it.

If your proposal deals with a potential cure for breast cancer, say so right away. Don't dance around the issue or talk about the technical ins and outs of the new gene therapy you hope will emerge from your project. Keep that part for later, and don't let it overshadow your main reason for seeking funding—a chance for a cure.

### Stress the benefit to the donor.

As in any sales pitch, you had better anticipate and have the answer to the ultimate and perfectly reasonable question, "What do I get out of all this?"

### Document your claims.

Don't make statements you can't back up with people or facts that prove your claim. Treat your material as something you have to take into court.

### Accentuate the positive.

Once you've stated the problem or opportunity, stress the upside of what you are doing. I even try to avoid words with negative contexts such as "never," "not," or "won't." Don't tell the prospect the school will close if he or she doesn't cough up. Say it will "once again be able to continue its vigorous tradition of providing well-trained, dedicated teachers for our elementary educational system."

Following this advice will give a fresh, vigorous feeling to your request that is missing from far too many proposals today. And don't forget, good luck is the residue of effort.

Let's take a look at a good way to tackle a major proposal and the material that should accompany it. Taken one by one, these ideas will help you avoid the pitfalls and booby traps that sink your competition. Everything I say that follows, of course, assumes that all the preliminary work in investigating and evaluating prospects, writing letters of inquiry, making follow-up phone calls, and visiting the prospect has already been taken care of. In other words, at this point, the prospect should be expecting to hear from you in detail.

## The three most important elements in any proposal package

Everything in a proposal is important, but some things are more important than others. These include the

- **cover letter** which will accompany your proposal,
- **summary** placed at or close to the beginning of the document, and
- **budget page** which may be an appendix or immediately follow the text.

## The cover letter

The cover letter should come from the highest ranking person in the organization submitting the proposal (president, executive director, trustee chairperson, etc.). It will clearly indicate the support of the parent organization and its leadership, and give the sender a chance to say nice things that might be inappropriate to have in the proposal itself. For example, it could remind the prospect of the excellent personal qualities and achievements of the principal parties involved, underscore the significance and impact the project would have on the day-to-day success on the organization submitting it, indicate the extent to which other prospects might be influenced by a favorable response by the donor, and grease the ways with "casual" remarks about mutual friends instrumental in getting the prospect and the submitter together. Get the picture? A good cover letter from the right sender to the right recipient can often move a proposal from the "to be read" pile to the "read now" pile. And that's a big step in itself.

## The summary

The summary is the next item of importance. In organizations besieged by hundreds or thousands of appeals, this may be the first (and sometimes, only) item read by the reviewer. In many cases, the reviewer will not have seen the cover letter. Consequently, the summary must capture the proposal's essence in just three or four paragraphs. On reading it, a person should immediately grasp what the project is, who the principal parties are, how much is needed and when, and what the benefit will be to the donor in particular and society in general.

## The budget page

The third and final item to focus on is the budget page. Once people have an idea what you want them to do, they want to know how you intend to use the money. A well-turned-out budget is the quickest way for them to find out. It tells them almost instantly how much thought has gone into planning the proposal. The better you can break out your costs, the more believable you will be. The budget page should be readable at a glance and clearly indicate all major categories, subtotals, and final total requested. In most cases, it need be no more than one page (the elements of a budget page may be seen below).

Give as much attention to the accuracy and clarity of the cover letter, the summary, and the budget page as you do to the rest of your proposal.

## Ten things every winning proposal has and what they do

Now that you know the three most important elements, let's see where they fit in with the other parts of a full proposal package. This package includes the following:

1. A cover letter
2. A title page
3. A table of contents
4. A summary
5. An introduction
6. A project description
7. Your organization's qualifications
8. A description of plans for evaluating the project
9. The "ask"
10. A budget page

27

Taking them one at a time, let's review the usefulness and significance of each of these items, three of which (1, 4, and 10) we have already discussed.

## The title page

The title page sets up what comes next. It provides core information to the prospective donor. A good one will always be clean, letter-perfect in appearance, and contain the following information. The words "A Proposal to" followed by the name of the person or agency to whom or which the proposal is directed. The next line should ask them "to Support" a specific project and tell them where this work will be carried out. The title page should also include your organization's full legal name and the name, address, and telephone number of the principal party responsible for receiving and administering the grant. It would look something like this.

A Proposal to
the XYZ Corporation
to Support the Children's Theater Program
at the Westville Community Center

The Westville Community Agency
June 15, 1991
Jill Black, Director
100 Center Street
Westville, PA 19000
(215) 123-4567

All this looks simple enough but often doesn't get done because submitters assume that the cover letter takes care of these details. But what happens when the cover letter gets separated or lost from the proposal, a not unusual event? This way the recipient immediately has a fair idea who you are, what you're after, and where you'll probably fall on their scale of funding priorities. If nothing else, it will help to get you a faster response if they turn you down. On the other hand, it will tell them where to go if they have points that need clarifying. (Interrogatory calls, by the way, are almost always a good sign.)

## The table of contents

List all section headings and appendix items here. The headings, in addition to dividing your proposal into manageable sections, should be used to convey essential information that can be taken in at a glance. Because of this, don't throw away the opportunity to score additional points by using bland subheads. Work as much drama and interest into them as you can without being silly. For example, Don't just say "introduction," if you're submitting a proposal to turn an old, abandoned movie theater into a shelter for the homeless. Say something like "Turning the Silver Screen into a Silver Lining" or "Finding a Picture-Perfect Answer for a Happy Ending." In other words, don't be boring. Each subhead should create interest and build on the one that preceded it. True, sometimes it just isn't possible or realistic to be clever, but you should always stretch for that little bit extra if you can. You can always go back and tone it down later.

The table of contents also serves as a useful checklist to make sure you've covered all the points you should, including the items that go into the appendixes.

## The introduction

Having mentioned the introduction, we may as well consider some of the things to say there. Only you will know exactly what this will be, but in a general sense be sure that you do this:

Put your organization in the "big picture." Where does your idea, project, or program fit in with what's being done elsewhere in the region. If it fits in with the statewide or nationwide picture, say so. If your outfit ranks right up there with the leaders in your field, don't be coy. Say so and back it up with the numbers or names to prove it. You can't expect the reviewer to run around tracking this vital information down. It's essential, too, that you not only establish a sense of where you fit in, but how you differ from the rest of the pack. Differentiating the product or service is as key for nonprofit fund raisers as it is for commercial advertisers and marketers. Maybe even more so. People have to eat and buy clothing and other consumer goods. They don't have to support charitable activities, cultural groups, or educational institutions.

The introduction is the place to state, in general terms, the societal needs or problems your project or idea will relieve or solve and what other kind of opportunities to advance the common good may exist in what you're trying to do. (Virtually all fund-raising appeals, by the way, are based on the "bad news-good news" principle, e.g., "The bad news is the world is going to hell; the good news is we've found a way to slow down the trip.")

The more people you can truthfully cite who will benefit from the funding of your proposal, the better chance you have of getting it funded. Don't exaggerate, but be persuasive or inspirational in a restrained, understated way. Base your proposal on the strengths of your organization and the opportunities your project provides. Never negotiate from weakness and need. It's a good idea, too, to point out what benefits will accrue to the prospect by taking part in your proposed venture. Often, these will take the form of "psychic income" (they'll feel good about it), but tangible rewards, such as having a building, a center, or an important post named for the donor or someone they wish to honor or putting a plaque up in their honor, are also possible. Usually, you need only cite how the donor will contribute to the public good over both the long and short term by taking part in your work. For smaller projects, local impact is a major selling point.

In simpler terms then, you're telling them about the current opportunity or problem, putting forth your solution to it (as far as it goes), and inviting them to share in the work. It's acceptable at this point to say how much you hope they will contribute and over what period of time. Leave the details, however, for the request section.

# The project description

Now we're moving from the general to the particular. This is where you spell out what you want to do in specific terms, why you want to do it now, and how you plan to do it. Here is where solid facts must speak for themselves. In simple terms, explain the main ideas step by step. You need not go into a "brick by brick" account, but you do need to tell them enough about what you are going to do and how you're going to do it so they can clearly retain the ideas and explain them to other persons without a struggle. (If you have a foundation or corporate officer on your side, a well-written proposal helps them sell your idea to the decision makers.) Tell them, too, how much planning has gone into your idea, what your timetable is for completing the project, and how much financial commitment there is from your membership, board of trustees, and staff to the venture's success. No one wants to be your sole source of inspiration and support for any project no matter how wealthy, well-endowed, or generous they are. If someone on your end feels that tedious and highly detailed matter, such as a scientific protocol, must be included in the proposal, put it in the appendix.

# Qualifications

Why are you the best outfit for this job? If you can't answer that question to your own satisfaction, you will have big trouble trying to sell your ideas to somebody else. Jot down four or five points that you think answer the question, pick out the best ones and elaborate on them. You may be better than you think. Most of us usually are.

When making your checklist for this section, include the personal qualifications and achievements of the people involved (provided, of course, that they apply to this project). Cite any special training they may have received, degrees held, particularly if from distinguished schools. Tell what kind of experience they have had that will insure the project's success. Talk about your facilities if they are good ones (or how a grant will improve them) and mention any existing equipment or technology you have that will be useful. Point out affiliations or working agreements you may have with other recognized groups or agencies in the field. Do you have access to consultants or advisors who can help? Persons on your board of directors, for instance.

If you, by some chance, are an organization just getting started you may not have the track record you'd like. That's okay. Be as honest and sincere as you can and you may win the day anyway. Enthusiasm counts.

# Evaluation

This is where you explain to the prospective donor how you intend to evaluate and report on the project's success once it is funded. Some foundations and corporations insist on at least one such report a year; others may want to receive one quarterly. Some funders may require an outside agency, often one they have selected, to evaluate the progress of your work. They may even go so far as to tell you exactly what they want to know and when they want to know it. Even if a report is not required, however, set your own deadline and standards for keeping your benefactors informed and involved. You may want to go back to them again. Most of us do. In fund raising as in sales, your best friends are the ones you already have.

Generally, your proposal's evaluation section can be understated and less specific than the others. The fact that you intend to do an analysis and report is usually sufficient at this point. The key phrase to keep in mind is "impact assessment." Donors want to know how much bang they're buying for their buck. It's your job to give them a fair, well-documented overview of what's up. But don't promise them more than you can deliver by way of analysis and evaluation.

Ideally, your report should reflect favorably on the progress of plans set forth in your proposal. If, for some reason, there should be a deviation from your timetable in terms of progress achieved or money spent (especially money spent), spell out what the snags are and how you intend to cope with them. Most donors are reasonable persons who want to see you get the job done. They will accept your cogent and timely explanation. At least the first time.

## Request

This is where you ask them for the money again. You will probably have already mentioned the amount sought in the summary, the introduction, and perhaps, even, the cover letter. Here, however, is where you restate your "ask" in slightly more detail. Here, too, you will sum up and remind them of key factors cited earlier. For example, you'll want to reiterate the project's significance and its local, state, and national impact, if any. (Redundancy serves the same purpose in fund-raising writing as it does in biology and physics. It increases the likelihood of an event taking place.) You'll want to list or mention other funds currently committed to the task, including those from your own organization and from important donors. Cite the project's total cost as given in the budget and say what part of this you hope your prospect will provide. In most instances, they won't want to be your sole source of support. If the project will last longer than the grant, tell them again how it will continue to be funded or pay for itself when the terms of the grant expire. One of the most important aspects of any successful appeal is the written assurance that at some point the program will fly on its own and not be continually or totally dependent on donations. Believe me, they don't want to adopt you.

You will also want to indicate how you intend to recognize the donors for their generosity. Will you put their name on the building, fund, or professorship? Will there be a plaque, an unveiling, or a dedication ceremony? Will the gift be publicized, with their approval? Recognition can be a selling point in itself.

In closing, remind them again how they will benefit as an individual or an organization by taking part in your work. Donor satisfaction is paramount. Then simply and directly ask them to award or give or grant you the specific amount you want over the exact time you will need it. Do you need $50,000 for the coming calendar year? Do you want or need $25,000 a year for the next three years? Just say it. Generally, three years is all you can reasonably expect a donor to share in your work. At that point the venture should be become self-sustaining. A one-year grant request is the norm. Donors are reluctant to be pinned down for more than that. (One way to get around short-term grants is to build a "request for renewal" in the stewardship report based on current progress.) Don't "respectfully request" anything or twist yourself into a pretzel trying to be sincere. If you haven't sold them on your idea by this time, tugging at the forelock won't help.

## The budget page

Increased competition for the corporate or foundation dollar has led donors to look at proposal budgets more closely than ever. The more detailed and specific you can be, the better chance your proposal will have to pass muster. Itemize things as much as possible. By the same token, your budget page should be able to be taken in at a glance. Divide your budget into capital expenses and operating expenses with subcategories under each. If you are requesting funds for more than one year, allow for inflation in each subsequent year.

### Capital expenses

Under this heading you can list space needs and equipment purchases or leases. Space needs will include costs for
- Construction
- Renovation
- Real estate purchases (Give total footage and costs per square foot.)
- Equipment purchase or lease can cover things like
  —Word processors
  —Computers
  —Copying machines
  —Office furniture
  —Laboratory equipment
  —Fax machines
  —Telephones
  —File cabinets
  —Any other hard goods you need

When you can, specify exact model numbers and how many of each item you will need.

### Operating expenses

This includes salaries and stipends, fringe benefits, office supplies, consultant's fees, licenses, fees, permits, insurance, utility costs, and miscellaneous expenses and contingency costs. Some things that qualify for support are salaries for principal investigators, administrators, support staff, secretaries, clerks, and technicians.

When considering office supplies and related costs, don't forget stationery, postage, advertising, publications, telephone, travel expenses, conference fees, books, periodicals, and audiovisuals.

Consultants' fees might mean architect's reports, feasibility studies, and engineering studies. Give the reasons for these.

Utility costs are the usual phone, gas, electric, and water bills we all get at home too.

Miscellaneous costs and expenses should always be clearly identified and explained.

**Overhead recovery**

Most private funding sources make no provision for this. A few do, however, so find out in advance if you may include it in your application and what the allowable percentage is.

These are just some of the items and just one approach to preparing your budget request. You might want to take a look at some of the models others are using and see if they'll work for you. Give your budget as much serious attention as you give to the other parts of your document.

## Supporting documents

Okay, your proposal is all written, checked, proofread, and approved. Is there anything else that belongs in the package? Of course. The IRS letter approving your 501 (c) (3) tax-exempt status. Put this and other material not appropriate for the main body of text in the appendixes to your proposal. This is the best place for resumes of key people, copies of your annual report, special charts and graphs, photographs, drawings, a history of the organization, and anything else that will strengthen your request and enhance your credibility.

## Check list

- [ ] Is this proposal a top priority for your organization?
- [ ] Have you made your main points clearly and effectively?
- [ ] Have you thoroughly researched this prospect and are you sure they will be interested in supporting this sort of venture?
- [ ] Does your opening command the reader's interest and curiosity?
- [ ] Have you focused on the people who will benefit from this grant?
- [ ] Is your language easy to read? Have you reduced or eliminated jargon?
- [ ] Did you include a summary of the main points, goals, and financial needs?
- [ ] Is there a positive and optimistic tone to your copy?

☐ Is your budget easy to read, yet comprehensive?

☐ Is your cover letter a winner and signed by your organization's highest official?

☐ Did you ask for the money in a clear and straightforward manner?

☐ Does your document look clean, well-structured, and professional?

☐ Are you sending your letter and proposal to *exactly the right person* at the corporation or foundation?

☐ Does your proposal and cover letter tell them who to call or write in response and where?

☐ Does your proposal clearly establish your outfit as the best one to support for the purpose stated?

☐ Have you shown how the granting agency or individual prospect will benefit from joining in or supporting your work?

☐ Have you made it clear that the prospect's support is needed now? Is there urgency in your request?

☐ Have you shown how you will support this effort in the future once the grant funding ends?

☐ Have you promised to evaluate and report on the effects of the grant on your organization's mission?

☐ Have you told the prospective donor how you will recognize the gift?

☐ Have you attached your 501 (c) (3) letter from the Internal Revenue Service?

☐ Does your appendix include resumes of key people, financial statements, annual reports, and other material supporting your request but not appropriate for the main body of text?

☐ Are you submitting *well ahead of the deadline*? Money runs out early sometimes, and even interested reviewers lose interest in plowing through hundreds of last-minute appeals.

## Exercises

• Using the reference materials you have gathered, draft an outline for an imaginary grant for a local nonprofit to one of the corporations or foundations you have contacted.

• Try to get a copy of a full proposal actually written and sent out by a local nonprofit, including the appendixes and cover letter. (You'll need a friend to help you get one.) Compare the approach they took with the guidelines in this chapter. What's missing?

- Rewrite the opening paragraph.
- Rewrite the summary (or make one if there isn't any). Which is better? Why?
- Draft a new cover letter for the proposal.
- Get a book on proposal writing from a public or university library that has sample proposals in it. Study them and compare their structure to the structure suggested here. Are they similar? Are they interesting?

# Chapter Five

# Writing Direct-mail Appeals

**T**HERE are many experts you can go to for insights into the value of direct mail and tips on how to write an effective appeal letter. Over the years, direct mail has moved in and out of fashion. Various approaches and packages are favored from time to time, and the arguments about what goes into a productive mailing seem to go on forever, usually coming back full circle from where they started. I'm not going to go into the nitty gritty about using demographics, good and bad rates of return, how often you should mail, list acquisition, planning a campaign, or the effects of rising postal costs. You can find that elsewhere and should do so if you're really serious about mastering the art. I'm simply going to tell you about points that absolutely must be covered by every fund-raising letter you write and what I think a minimum direct-mail package should contain. In principle, these things are simple. In practice, they can, and should be, quite time-consuming. The reasons most direct mail appeals fail are two-fold: **1)** the writer doesn't devote enough time to planning the piece; and **2)** he or she fails to write and revise the letter from the reader's point of view.

## The virtues of a good letter

If you have never done a direct-mail appeal, there are some things about its advantages you should know before you begin. First of all, according to direct-mail wizard Jerry Huntsinger, a good direct-mail letter ranks second only to a face-to-face chat with the prospect. When he or she opens your letter, you've got your prospect all alone and, if you've done your job well, you've got his or her full attention. Because you choose how you tell your story and who will and who won't get your letter, you can zero in on persons you are reasonably sure have a good reason to support your organization or who, at least, are well disposed toward it. Things are pretty much in your control. (It is crucial not to blow this advantage.) Another favorable point is, that in spite of constant increases in postal rates, a direct-mail appeal will still be the cheapest, most effective way to reach your audience. You get a big impact for a relatively low unit cost.

A final point you should consider, no matter how many newspaper or magazine articles you read about the curse of "junk mail" is this: there is no such thing as "junk mail." People love to get letters of any kind as long as they are interesting. A well-designed, well-timed, well-written direct-mail piece can brighten many a day. If you don't think this is true, let someone else write your appeal letters.

## The purpose of direct mail

In fund raising, there are two kinds of direct mail. One helps you build your prospect base by adding new donors and uncovering potential new major donors. The other aims at increasing your cash flow by keeping old donors aboard and getting them to upgrade their gifts. Sometimes both aims can be accomplished at once but not usually. What you're trying to accomplish, i.e., goal #1 or goal #2, will influence what you say and how you say it. A letter seeking first-time contributions will have a different feel than a letter asking persons to make larger gifts or give more than once a year. (As a general principle, it's good practice to have no more than one main theme to a letter. It only confuses readers if they have to grasp too many ideas. This theme might be asking them to "join a winning team," or "offer new hope to parents of autistic children." Everything else in your letter must support your main theme and build toward an irresistible ask.)

## Make your first sentence count

A letter can have a good or a bad opening. It better be a good one or you're already dead, headed for the circular file with other poorly planned, poorly written appeals. But how can you know whether you're got a good or a bad opening? It's not so hard, really.

**1.** First of all, your first sentence should be **short**. No more than ten or eleven words if you can manage it. (Copywriting expert Herschel Gordon Lewis calls this principle his "Canon No. 1.")

2. It will have the word "**you**" in it.
3. It will be about something of **compelling personal interest** to the reader.
4. It will sound **true**.
5. It will promise a **benefit** to the reader.

Sounds like a lot to accomplish in ten or eleven words doesn't it? Getting all these points across in a single sentence won't be easy, but it's not impossible, and the closer you come, the better you'll do.

The first sentence might resemble something like "You can make $5,000 for just five minutes work," or "You are one of just 100 persons eligible for free membership." These are just crude examples, of course, but if you received such a letter, wouldn't you read the next sentence? And the next? And the next? The answer will always be yes if the writer's focus continues to be on the reader and not the sender. Like the old song, your refrain should be "You, you, you, I'm in love with you, you, you." The reason Lewis and others suggest that you keep your first, attention-grabbing sentence short is because it will make the letter seem easy to read all the way through. (In fact, the letter better be easy to read all the way through.) Long first sentences turn readers off. One of your copy-revising and proofreading skills should be a keen eye for removing visual or mental roadblocks for the reader. Make it as easy as possible for them to understand what it is you want them to do and how you want them to do it. And all along, you must be moving the reader from thought to action.

## The Form of a Good Letter

Once you have your readers' interest, keep them hooked by injecting an element of mystery in your copy. Try not to give your story away before the end. Your letter should have a beginning, a middle, and an end just like any other story. To make sure this happens, certain elements must be in place.

- **Put a date on the letter**—so people will know that it's a recent, timely appeal and not one sent out blindly. Without a date, your letter is really just a flier or another form of brochure.
- **Give some thought to the salutation**. If you're lucky enough to have computer capabilities for dropping in first names or nicknames, you're well ahead of the game. If, however, this is not an option, general openings such as "Dear Friend," "Dear Graduate," or "Dear Fellow Artist" are perfectly acceptable.

The main point is that the salutation immediately include the reader in a select, even elite, group of real people. Try to greet the readers as what or how they perceive themselves. We all play many roles in life; seek the most appropriate for this appeal. Don't begin the letter, as many do, with only the copy itself. It looks wrong. It is wrong.

- **The body of copy, the heart of your sales pitch, should accomplish four things**—which are easily remembered by the memory device, AIDA. AIDA isn't the name of an opera by Verdi here, however, it stands for Attention, Interest, Desire, and Action. Attention is what you get with that first sentence; Interest has to be created by the story you have to tell; Desire is stimulated as the reader realizes that something can be done only with his or her help and support; and finally, you must spur them to Action by asking them to act now. Send a check or money order. Call the number below. (We'll talk about what the key elements are for this "action" section of the letter later.)

- **Sign off**. Every letter should have a complimentary close. And just one. Don't fall into the common error of closing a letter with a double complimentary close. By this I mean don't let your last sentence be "With all best wishes," followed by "Yours truly," or "Sincerely yours," and a signature. The last sentence of an effective letter will always be a full sentence constituting a complete thought and ending in a period or some other punctuation mark. Otherwise, you've just thrown away a fine opportunity to close on a high note, add a word of thanks or inspiration, or remind the reader of some important point that needs to be stressed more then once. Never waste words in a fund-raising letter. Make everything you say count to the fullest in achieving your goal of having the reader make as large a contribution to your cause as possible—as quickly as possible.

- **The signature is important**. When most persons open a letter, it's the first thing they look at after their own name. That's why your letter should be signed by the highest-ranking person in the organization: the president, the chief executive officer, or the chairperson of the board. (And for heaven's sake, don't let the signer get the idea that he or she should actually write the letter. Some of them do, you know, and it's always a disaster.) Don't use celebrity signatures unless there is a clear connection between the celebrity and what you and your organization do. People give to ideas and opportunities, not celebrities. In some cases, I think ill-advised celebrity signatures put people off, actually losing potential gifts. Letters signed by wealthy persons, for instance, seem to have that effect on me. I mean, why don't *they* ask them for the money?

- **The P.S.** Everybody reads this. Use it to get an important special message across that might get in the way of the regular copy, for example, "To be eligible for this year's tax deduction, your gift must be received before December 31." or "The first 1,000 gifts will receive a free desk calendar."

## The Essential Contents

So, now that we've covered the six things that must be in a good letter (date, salutation, body of copy, complimentary close, signature, and P.S.), let's take a closer look at point three, what goes into the body of copy. How can you be sure that you will get their attention, create interest, motivate desire, and inspire them to action? Think of five W's and two H's.

## The five "W's"

Use the five "W's" taught to first-year journalism students: Who, What, When, Where, and Why. Never assume, even when writing to alumni or close friends of the organization, that they know who you are and what you want.

- **Tell the reader who you are**. The name of your organization and what you're in business for.
- **Tell the reader what you want them to support**. The more specific you can be, the better luck you'll have. Just crying poor ain't gonna make it. That only drops you down to the panhandler level. You've got some exciting programs going and some real opportunities to promote change, increase literacy, give kids confidence, or alleviate loneliness and despair. Whatever it is that got you interested in your nonprofit's activities will get your donors interested too. Tell them about it. To make your message even clearer, underline key words and sentences and set off a series of three or more important points with "bullets." If the letter runs more than one page, and some do, use subheads to break up copy, provide transition, and create interest.
- **Tell the reader when you need the gift**. A deadline lends urgency. You need it now! You need it yesterday! The sooner you get it, the more it will do! Anything you do to create and reinforce a sense of urgency will increase your chances of getting a new gift from first time donors and a bigger gift from existing donors.

- **Tell the reader why he or she should support you**. This is where you use your story line to its fullest advantage. Are you doing the best job in this field? In your community? Is your track record good? With the least cost? Can you offer testimonials from satisfied customers, clients, or beneficiaries? (If so, please do. Your letter's believability will triple.) Are you a leader or pioneer in the field? Are you a true innovator? Do you provide special services to a particularly cut-off or needy segment of society? Are you a point of light? Tell them about it.
- **Tell them where to send the money**. One of the cardinal sins of well-meaning volunteer groups is forgetting to include the address and telephone number of the people who will receive, record, and acknowledge the gift in the letter. (Prompt receipts and thank you notes are important too. More on this in the stewardship section.) Make sure you put all the necessary response information *in the appeal letter* that you have on the return device, be it a pledge card or RSVP invitation. Never assume that such things don't get separated or lost. For safety's sake, you could even include response information on the back of the envelope. That would list it in three easy-to-find places. If they don't know where to send the gift, you're not going to get it.

Some current direct-mail experts have urged asking for the gift up front in the letter—in the first paragraph or two. I disagree. We should have more to say about what we do than "we need money." Asking for the gift up front also means the letter itself is just a sham. You have to offer more than that. When I was in Chicago's financial district recently, a panhandler asked me for a handout. As I walked away, he said, "I'm a Republican, too." The laugh he got earned him a buck. Just asking for the gift doesn't make it these days. You've got to have style and substance.

## The two H's

The following points are the two most important in writing direct mail appeals. Remember these, and all else will follow!

- **Tell them how much you want them to give, or how much you want them to increase their gift over last time**. (Don't remind them that they haven't given lately. Tell them, instead, how valuable their past support has been.) List the biggest dollar amount first if there are more than one. "We hope you will consider a gift of $250 or more", or "Won't you give $250, $175, or $100 to help these children?" If you don't ask for the big numbers, you'll never get them. But somebody else might.

- **Tell the readers how they will benefit from making this gift and supporting your cause**. Everybody likes to feel good about themselves, to know that they've just done something special. Will the donor be listed on your honor roll, get a free subscription to your newsletter, be invited to future events? Tell them, and tell what a difference their gift will make in your special world and the world in general. Tell them how wonderful they are. There's no such thing as too much flattery. As the late actress, Tallulah Bankhead is supposed to have said, "The hell with criticism, I'll settle for good old-fashioned praise."

## What makes a good package

We've been talking quite a bit about "the letter," but a letter should never be sent off on its lonesome. For obvious reasons, every letter has to go out in an envelope. Today, the envelope itself has become an art form, not least because the United States Postal Service keeps adding restrictions about size, cost, what you can and can't put on them, and where everything has to go. Given rising first-class and bulk-mail rates, the envelope is much too important an element to be wasted or, at least, under-used. Design is the critical issue. What should your envelope look like? Should it be standard or nonstandard size? Should it have a window? Should it have a "teaser" on the front to make sure people will want to open it? Should the address be typed, a label, or written by hand? Should the letter have a stamp or an indicia? All interesting points that have to be worked out for each organization and each package.

I've seen items that looked like telegrams, interoffice envelopes, official U.S. Government business, surveys, questionnaires, and plain brown wrapping paper. What next? Whatever form you choose, the envelope should "look" like your organization and reflect the nature and character of its work. If you have a symbol or slogan, be sure it shows.

- The most important part of the package, of course, is what we have just spent most of this chapter on. A warm, one-on-one letter from one good person (me) to another good person (you).
- Every well-planned fund-raising letter should also have an enclosure. Usually this will be a pledge card (with all important information from the letter repeated) and a reply envelope to make it easier and faster to get their gift off to you. The pledge card and the reply envelope, incidentally, should be a different color, if only slightly so, from the letter so they stand out and

are easy to find. And you need not put a stamp on the reply envelope. Let that be one of the donor's "contributions." Other items that might be sent along from time to time as enclosures are newsletters, brochures, or some inexpensive premium such as a calendar or memo-and-address book.

## Dealing with complaints

Everyone who writes and distributes a piece of direct mail asking for someone's support is sticking his or her neck out. Lurking out there in the great unknown are individuals who will pounce on your message and use it as a basis for airing their own private griefs and complaints against the organization. When this happens, panic often sets in with administrators or board members. Horrendous law suits are envisioned. Everybody will hate us for asking for money! Our biggest donor probably feels the same way, but hasn't said anything! Our prospect base will dry up and blow away!

Probably not. Unless there are dozens or hundreds of such letters (in which case you may really have a problem somewhere in the organization), the best thing to do is file them away for future reference. You need not reply to any but the most specific complaints, and even then, you need go no farther than to thank them for informing you of the problem and helping you to improve your services. Whatever you do, don't get into a prolonged correspondence with these people. They'll love it and you'll be driven to distraction as you sink deeper into muck without any hope of resolving things. Think of complaint letters or calls as acceptable casualties in the battle for support. Everybody has them. Never despair. Even a bad fund-raising letter will raise more money than no letter at all.

## Check list

- [ ] Is your first sentence short? Less than 10 or 11 words?
- [ ] Is the word "you" in it?
- [ ] Is it interesting, compelling, or intriguing?
- [ ] Does it promise a benefit?
- [ ] Is it *true*?
- [ ] Is there a story to your letter or are you just piling up facts?
- [ ] Did you date the letter?
- [ ] Does the salutation identify the reader in a way he or she recognizes and likes?
- [ ] Did you follow the AIDA principle in structuring your letter?
- [ ] Is there *just one* complimentary close?

☐ Did the right person sign the letter?

☐ Did you use the P.S. effectively to get a special point across?

☐ Did you say *who* you (the organization) are and what you do?

☐ Did you tell them *what* you want them to support and *why*?

☐ Did you tell them *when* you need the gift?

☐ Did you say *where* to send the money?

☐ Did you tell them *how much* (or how much more) you hope they will give?

☐ Is there a response device and return envelope?

☐ Are the pledge card and return envelope a different color than the letter?

☐ Do the letter and the pledge card *both* have the same basic information about how much to give and where to send it?

☐ Did you tell them *how* they will benefit from supporting you?

☐ Does your direct mail package look like your organization and what it does?

☐ Did you talk more about the donor (you) than the organization (we)?

# Exercises

- Read at least one book on the principles of direct mail solicitation.

- Save all the direct mail solicitations you receive for a month. Analyze and compare the styles of the packaging—envelope, return device, and letter set-up. Which appeal to you most? Which the least? Can you tell why?

- Pick out one of the letters that most closely resembles the format suggested in this chapter. How many points match up? Was the first sentence a winner? Was it short or long? Was the copy convincing? Were key elements highlighted? Did you know who the person was who signed the letter? Was there a P.S.?

- Which letters didn't you open right away? Why? What was the reason you weren't interested?

- Take what, in your view, are the worst two or three letters and rewrite them according to the guidelines in this chapter. How do they look now?

Chapter Six

# Writing Effective Stewardship Letters and Reports

**W**HAT do a multimillion-dollar gift and a $5 donation have in common? They both deserve a prompt, personal acknowledgment. The purpose of stewardship is to get the next gift. Saying "thanks" fast and often is the best way you have of hanging on to your present supporters and establishing a relationship that will lead to bigger or more frequent gifts later on. A simple receipt with an expression of gratitude such as "Thanks for making our day," and signed by the organization's treasurer will do. The point is to get the acknowledgment out within seven days of receiving the gift. You will be amazed at how effective this is in setting up renewed gifts or making donors more agreeable to increasing this year's donation over last year's. Retaining and upgrading donors is the heart and soul of any direct mail appeal but is even more true in the case of corporate and foundation supporters. With major donors, more than a receipt is usually involved. If gifts move above a certain benchmark, whether it's $1,000 or $25,000, you'll need to send a letter from your president or director of development (or both) and some sort of stewardship accounting somewhere down the road. This could be anything from a gift recognition book or once-a-year newsletter to a five- or ten-page, single-spaced personal report replete with charts, tables, and diagrams. Stewardship means staying in touch. All the time. Not just when you're gearing up for another appeal or about to launch a campaign. In some fund-raising operations, even at large universities or nonprofit associations, stewardship only gets a lick and a promise; at others, it doesn't get done at all which is not only sad, but highly counterproductive.

In a small shop, the problem usually rests in not enough hands being available to do follow-up projects. People are so busy taking care of asking for money, they just haven't got time to stop and thank those who come through with it. In this context, the more you can do to automate your receipting and thank-you letters, the better. By "automate" I don't necessarily mean using computers to track gifts and send out acknowledgments, I just mean doing all you can to simplify the process. Developing a standard prepackaged receipt form that lets you write in the donor's name and amount without fuss will do fine. Don't worry, by the way, about sending out the same format all the time. The donor doesn't really care. He or she just want to be recognized while they're still basking in the afterglow of generosity. It's the quick response that keeps this spark alive in between appeals.

## The stewardship letter as a minimalist art form

A stewardship letter need not be complicated. In addition to a date (very important), a salutation as personal as is appropriate (Dear Dick, Dear Jane, Dear Dr. Doe, etc.), a complimentary close, and a signature it only needs to:

1. **Immediately thank the donor** for his or her generosity, thoughtfulness, vision, kindness, leadership, inspiration, encouragement (you can see where I'm going, can't you?) without overdoing it;
2. **Tell them how useful**, timely, appropriate, fitting, etc., the gift is;
3. **Indicate how it will be used**;
4. **Add a bit of new information about the organization** (optional) including, perhaps, an appropriate bit of history, a reference to recent developments, or some hint at future plans. Always try to leave them knowing a bit more about you than before. Bind them to your heart; and
5. **Thank the donor again** on behalf of any others who may be affected by the gift, including those not in a position to do so for themselves (trustees, staff, clients, students, patients, etc.).

When you get this procedure down, it will be a snap to bat out dozens of letters a day by simply varying the content a bit or interchanging words and phrases. You're not going after a Pulitzer Prize here, you just want to get the thank-you letter on its way.

## The stewardship report and how to feed it

Stewardship reports, like proposals and letters, have basic elements that must be included for your message to be clear, concise, and complete. These are:

- A title page
- The background of the grant
- A summary of the entire report
- The body of the report
- A conclusion
- A financial statement
- A cover letter

Let's see why we need all seven of these elements and what should go into each one.

**The title page** establishes the tone of the report. It immediately shows how important the donor and the gift are to your organization. It should also include the month and the year it is being submitted. It need say no more than something like "A report to Mrs. John Doe on the restoration of Woodland Arboretum" followed by the date of submittal. The grant number, if there is one, should be included when reporting to corporations and foundations.

**The background of the grant** should mention the size and duration of the grant, when you received it, and what you received it for. In essence, you will simply repeat what was said to you in the donor's original letter awarding you the funds. You have to do this in each report because the reviewer may not be the person who made the grant in the first place. Even if he or she is, they probably won't have a copy of the original grant in front of them or even close at hand. A reminder like this is both helpful and courteous.

**Summarize** the gist of your report in three or four sentences. Reviewers may not have time to read the whole thing if it's one of many that came in that week. You'll gain points by making things easy for them.

In **the body of your report**, elaborate on the summary. Describe what progress you've made to date or since you filed your last report. These things should correspond closely with the aims and goals that you laid out in your original grant request. People get very nervous if you're not doing the things you said you were going to do or if you're doing them in a different sequence or on a different scale. If you have strayed afield from what you originally told your donor, be prepared to justify this. Convincingly. It's important that you high-light and expand on key developments. Be sure, too, to cite any spe-cial benefits that may have resulted above and beyond the original purpose of the request such as other grants received, honors given, seminars held, lectures delivered, or books and articles published. In other words, anything good that has happened since you first got your money.

Use simple language to do this. It's only a progress report, so the simpler and clearer the better. Break up the copy with headings and subheadings when you can. Long gray stretches of copy are bleak and numbing, even more so if yours is the twenty-fifth or thirtieth report of the week (or day, in some cases). Use "bullets," "boxes," and charts or graphs if you've got them.

In your **conclusion**, explain the significance of the progress (or lack of it) that you've just described. Tell them what will happen next, and outline the steps you will probably take in doing this. Let them know what your future expectations are, too, whether this is your first or your last report. Donors appreciate a sense of continuity in things they've helped to get started.

Stewardship reports should always include a **financial statement** that details how the money's been spent up to this point. It should be signed by the chief financial auditor whether it is one of the Big Eight accounting firms or your brother-in-law who happens to be a CPA.

Finally, draft a **cover letter** from the person who signed the origi-nal grant proposal cover letter. This is another chance to thank the donor again and say how grateful you still are for all his or her help.

Do these things and your donor will not only be grateful but con-vinced that you are managing your grant responsibly and thoughtful-ly. It could pave the way for submitting another successful request down the line.

# Thanking them "seven times"

It has often been said that you should thank every donor "at least seven times." Who first came up with this biblical-sounding admoni-tion, I don't know, but what he or she was really saying was never pass up an opportunity to let you donors know how vital they are to your success. What are these seven things you can do?

- First of all, there is the receipt you mail after getting the gift. Does it say "Thank you" somewhere? It should.
- Second, you can send them a personal thank-you note from one of your key people.
- Third, you can call them personally to thank them right away.

- Fourth, you can include their names on your annual "honor role" of donors published in your newsletter, annual report, or gift book.
- Fifth, you can send them an inexpensive "premium" of some kind such as a donor pin, calendar, or your newsletter.
- Sixth, you can invite them to one of your special events such as a reception, opening, lecture, or performance.
- Seventh (see how fast we got there), if the gift is a large one, you can send out a news release or tip off one of the donor's local papers, TV, or radio stations. (Send the donor a draft of the release for approval and clearance first, but set a hard deadline for its return.)

You can also report the gift in your in-house periodicals, cite the donor in reports to other agencies (such as NIH) or have a luncheon in the donor's honor.

I won't go on. I'm sure you can think of some other thank-you opportunities on your own, such as acknowledging their presence at meetings or receptions, sending them a greeting card, or asking their advice about your fund-raising plans. Whatever else you do, keep them in touch and involved with your organization's future.

## The marketing benefits of gift books and annual reports

What's the first thing you do when you get a stewardship publication from an organization that you've supported this year? You look up the list of donors to see:

1. That *you're* included.
2. That *your name* is spelled right and listed in the right donor category.
3. *Who else gave* that you know, or who is prominent in the community.

Donors love company.

You've sent out a gift book or newsletter. Now that you have your donor's attention, don't throw away the opportunity to tell him or her more about your organization and its plans. Interesting photographs and captions linked to fund-raising successes, needs, or opportunities provide you with an excellent chance to plant new information in the mind of the donor, kindle new interest in your special efforts, and acknowledge the significance of private support to your success. A brief letter or editorial from your chief executive can highlight the year's successes in terms of dollars raised, needs addressed, and leading sources of support. If you had more donors last year, tell them. If your average gift went up 20 percent, tell them. If you just got the biggest gift you ever got, tell them. Donors love to stick with winners, and there is always a way to put a positive spin on your story. If *you* don't tell them how great you're doing and how vital they are to your success, who do you think will?

These reports and gift books can be done inexpensively for the most part. They can range from simple donor lists inserted in other publications to Xeroxed copies of a single, computer-produced piece or low-budget booklets printed in one or two colors. (I'm always fascinated by what a trained designer can achieve with minimal resources.)

I'll say it again. The best donors you have are the ones you have right now. Do all that you can to keep them and upgrade their gifts. Be a good and faithful steward. It's the only way to turn an endless courtship into a solid marriage.

## Check list

- ☐ Do you have a formal structure for triggering thank-you notes and stewardship reports?
- ☐ Are donors being thanked within a week of receiving their gifts?
- ☐ Does your letter point out the significance of the gift and say how it might be used?
- ☐ Does your letter offer new information about your organization and the work it is doing?
- ☐ Have you thanked the donor on behalf of those who will benefit most from the gift?
- ☐ Does your stewardship report have the seven basic components that assure completeness and convey a sense of organizational competence?
- ☐ Have you included background information on the grant (when you got it, how much, what for, and for how long) in your report?
- ☐ Does your report summarize progress to date up front?
- ☐ Does your conclusion satisfy any questions a reviewer may have about future efforts or results?
- ☐ Did you include an up-to-date, audited financial statement of expenditures?
- ☐ Have you made efforts to thank donors in other ways?
- ☐ Have you listed all this year's donors in your gift book, honor roll, or annual report?

☐ Did you spell their names right?

☐ Did your letter ask them to consider moving up to a higher gift level in the future?

## *Exercises*

- Ask five or six local nonprofits for samples of their gift receipts. Colleges, hospitals, United Way, the Boy and Girl Scouts, the American Cancer Society, and American Heart Association, for example, will be happy to send you theirs. Tell them you are doing a study.

- Keep any stewardship-related material you may receive such as donor acknowledgment lists, gift books, newsletters, etc. You will be surprised at the frequency with which these appear.

- Compare items of the same type with one another. Are they attractive? Interesting? Informative? Expensive looking? Which do you like best? Why?

- Save all the stewardship items you receive from an organization you support for a calendar year. How many of the items reflect the advice in this chapter? Were you thanked seven times?

- Check the donor lists. How many people did you know at least by name? Which leadership group did you feel you should belong to? Did you?

- Volunteer to put together a stewardship package for one of your local nonprofit agencies or assist with their current program. You'll learn plenty from the experience, not all of it about writing.

# Chapter Seven

# Writing Specialty Items — Mission and Case Statements, Campaign Plans, and Position Papers

**F**OR the novice, and even for the professional fund-raising writer, certain tasks fall within the realm of the mysterious. I refer here to mission and case statements. Unless you work for a consulting firm or an agency who deals with a large number of nonprofit groups or happen to be a freelancer specializing in these things, you will rarely have to write one. So, when they do come up, most of us have to stop and think a moment about how to do them. Far too often we tend to grind out copy-cat pieces that fail to do what these things are intended to do—*clearly set our organization, its activities, and its needs and opportunities apart from those of similar organizations competing with us for the same fund-raising dollar.* Often, where one organization's purpose is similar to that of another's, such as a college or university, for example, you could substitute one name for another in some of these pieces without anyone being the wiser. What I will try to do here is show you how to approach these misunderstood tools in a way that will insure your mission statement or case statement works for your cause and yours alone.

## The mission statement

A mission statement is somewhat like a political platform. It talks about, and in some way defines, what your nonprofit stands for. These are invariably good and desirable things that are as acceptable to everyone as more effective education, better health, and lower taxes.

Some charitable foundations and corporations ask you to include a mission statement in your proposals, but most don't require one. Nor, for that matter, do many nonprofits take the trouble to draft one. That's not surprising, because, while simple in principle, setting forth the elements of an organization's mission can be complex and politically explosive. For this reason, deciding what should be included in such a statement and how much stress each element should get should be discussed by the organization's key officers in advance of a draft. If your organization's people are really interested in the mission statement, they will squabble over what should or shouldn't be in it and exactly how things should be stated. Usually, once the facts are in place, the writing task will then be handed over to a development, public relations or marketing writer or to someone else whose editorial skills will assure that the statement is not only clear and effective, but also has a little "poetry' to it. But the final statement should be written under the aegis of the executive director, chief operating officer, or president.

## The necessary ingredients

Writing a mission statement should be approached with care, because this document will provide a platform from which to draw the conclusions that will shape the character of your case statement. As someone said long, long ago, "let your mission state your case." On the other hand, mission statements need not be carved in stone but updated from time to time to conform with your organization's changing activities and goals.

To be effective, a mission statement must achieve the following things:

- Give clues to your institution's character
- Reveal its philosophy
- State its objectives and reason for being

The institution's community role and state or national influence should be clear, if this is, indeed, the case.

The most famous mission statement in American history is the short, graceful, and precise preamble to the Constitution of the

United States:

"...in order to form a more perfect union, establish justice, insure domestic tranquillity, provide for the common defense, promote the general welfare, and secure the blessings of liberty to ourselves and our posterity..."

These six wonderful points that have been sufficient to guide the world's most powerful organization are model enough for us all. They also show the value of checking back with your mission statement when your organization wanders off track from time to time.

The final mission statement must be acceptable to the board of trustees and the senior staff, because a primary internal function of the mission statement is to prevent misunderstandings or disagreements about fund-raising and other organizational goals.

## Keep it simple

For some organizations, the attempt at a mission statement is often an institutional first. The bewilderment invariably arising from such attempts underscores how few organizations really have a clear idea about where they are supposed to be going. For this reason, first drafts can tend to ramble on and become overlong, wordy, and pretentious. Big stuff calls for big words, right?

Wrong.

After you finish your first draft, take an axe to it. Go back and take out as many adjectives and adverbs as you can, find a shorter version for all the nouns and verbs you can, and break big paragraphs into little ones. Try to fit the thing onto a single, double-spaced page or page-and-a half at most. I say this because, like Abraham Lincoln's famous *Gettysburg Address*, your mission statement should get to the heart and soul of the issues. And it should do so in a way that is easily retained. (To this day, no one remembers a word of what Edward Everett, the principal speaker at the dedication of Gettysburg National Cemetery said. And he spoke for two-and-half hours.)

When you get around to writing your mission statement, set firm deadlines for all discussions, comments, and final review. Otherwise, writing the statement will drag on and on and become irritating to your leadership. Make them get on with it so they can use it as soon as possible.

## The case statement

As you can see, mission statements tend to be philosophical. Case statements, on the other hand, must be more visionary and action-oriented. The case statement justifies your campaign to the reader. If it works, it will inspire him or her not only to support you with their own gifts, but to act as your advocate with others. Winning hearts and minds is essential to success.

The case statement can:

- Gain public and internal support for the campaign;
- Serve as a resource for all subsequent letters, speeches, brochures, news releases, proposals, and other documents; and
- Break the ice on visits with key prospects, committee members, trustees, and others;
- Be left behind for study and consideration by the prospect and set the stage for another call or visit.

Other writers in the organization will frame their proposals and appeals in terms of the "party line" set forth by the case statement, and it will arm volunteer solicitors with facts and figures that will help them to convince donors that yours is the cause for them.

## Some common problems that may hinder the effectiveness of your case statement

**1. Getting agreement on the case statement's purpose, priorities, and funding needs.** Mission statements can help lay the groundwork here, but it's vital to pin down these details before you go to work. What you need, when you need it, and why you need it, complete with price tags, must be decided by the campaign leadership and set forth as part of a written campaign plan (see below). This can be a tricky task if you're dealing with persons unfamiliar with the ins and outs of fund raising. Busy executives and trustees can be elusive and vague if not pressed on these matters. Usually, the delays here result from having to decide in favor of one element of an organization over another and the political fallout that may result. Still, it has to be done.

**2. Getting the case statement written by the right person is another major consideration.** Committees can't inspire readers or give the proper focus or slant to large masses of information and ideas. It takes a skilled writer to sort it out and write a persuasive, moving document that speaks with a single voice. How you say it is just as important as what you have to say.

**3. Getting a clean, contemporary look to the design.** The best copy in the world can't find its way through a poorly designed or overdesigned case statement. Even if your piece is only produced on a typewriter, there are ways to make it look better and easier to read (see Chapter 13: The Value of Good Design).

**4. Getting the right people to read it.** Sit down and discuss the constituency you serve and the audience you are aiming at before you actually write your piece. Since one of the campaign's chief purposes is to broaden your constituency of supporters and advocates, you'll need to think hard about distributing it to a larger audience than usual. Do legislators, city officials, and social or political activists figure in your future plans in some way? Maybe they should get a copy. What about key members of your own community or civic associations? Prospects and donors need not, indeed, should not, be the only targets for your case. Those who do read your case, by the way, will really be interested in what it has to say. All the more reason that what it says should accurately reflect a true sense of your organization or institution and the wishes of its leaders. You might want to consider having two or three major donors review your draft and comment on content and thrust. You needn't be bound by their views, but they can sometimes be helpful.

## An approach to writing the case statement

Get your reader's attention immediately. Start out with a truly interesting, challenging, or arresting statement or question. Lead them into the copy in a way that will force them to pursue the thread of your main idea to its logical, convincing, and inspiring conclusion. Write, therefore, the best lead sentence and paragraph of which you are capable. Virtually everything depends on its success.

How do you do this? Well, you'll never do it by being stuffy. There's a wonderful account in an essay by George Orwell of working-class English men and women sitting glumly in a pub in 1940 listening to the Oxbridge tones of the BBC radio announcer drone on and on about the evacuation of Dunkirk. Then the cockney voice of one of the rescued soldiers came through the speaker. Instantly, every head in the pub jerked up in unison to listen eagerly to one of their own. They had been touched where they live. This is what you're after. Only officials love the sound of the official voice.

- **Create and build interest as you go along**. Establish premises. If this, if that, if the other be true, then what follows? Make points. Point one. Point two. Point three. Elaborate on them. Make the reader anxious to see what you are leading up to and to hear your conclusions. While doing this, remember that you must make your case bigger than your agency or institution. For instance, if you are a medical school, you might focus on the politicalization of health care or the declining (or rising) interest in medicine as a profession and all this implies for the future of America's health care system. This would then set up a discussion of your role in dealing with the problem and what some of your proposed contributions to its solution might be. From there, you will go on to citing how donors can expedite things and assure a successful outcome. Remember the old Hollywood formula for making a successful film? Boy gets girl. Boy loses girl. Boy gets girl. (Or vice versa.) People need a story with a happy ending. Don't let them down.

- **Build confidence in the reader's mind as you write.** Outline your action plan clearly and use analogies and metaphors that will help the reader recall its basic concepts and ideas. Is there a team approach? Is there a pyramid of steps to follow. Are there waves of activity? If you've done the job right, the reader should be able to use such devices to summarize the contents of your case and tick off the key details to another person without difficulty. This should be one of the aims you strive for. Make it possible for others to convey your message for you after reading the case. You'll need to show all the planning and thought that has gone into your campaign, but without necessarily giving a blow-by-blow account. Above all, talk about the people who will make it work. Put a human face on what you're trying to do. People relate to people. And when you draw your conclusions it will be essential, in closing, to convince your readers of the permanent benefits your successful campaign will yield to them, the community, and society in general. Underscore, too, the satisfaction, recognition, and prestige they will enjoy from having been part of it all.

- **At some point, after you have described the general situation, give a breakdown of what kind of funding is needed—** for each part of your case and where you expect it to come from. Indicate to donors and prospects that they will not be alone in supporting your cause. Show institutional or organizational commitment to the campaign's success including anticipated gifts from trustees, staff, and employees. Mention the size of your nucleus fund—all the advance gifts (usually about a third of what you hope to raise) already committed to the campaign. This makes it easier for prospects to buy in to your goals.

Because 20 percent of your donors will provide 80 percent of the gifts you need, assign specific dollar amounts to all areas targeted for support. the big number first, then break it down into examples of what some of its components may be. If you seek $5 million for a new community theater, tell them how much will go for construction, staff salaries, lighting, sound systems, costume and scenery shops, a green room, and so on. Whet their appetite as you set the table by briefly explaining some of the interesting points about each of these elements.

- **Tell your donors exactly what you want them to do**—and when you want them to do it. Stress the urgency of getting major gifts now and not at some vague time in the future. Let the donor know that the sooner a gift or grant is received the more valuable and productive it will be. (It will get a program up and running sooner. More people will be reached. Costs will be less.) Include a number donors can call or Fax or an address they can write to. At all times, make it as easy as you can for a person to step forward and join the team.

- **Be positive, optimistic, and enthusiastic in your writing**— but, at the same time, be aware that understatement always works better than exaggeration. If your message is sincere, it will get across better without editorializing or purple prose. Your goal is to create interest and enthusiasm in the mind of the reader for helping to meet the challenge. Tell them your dream, then ask them to share in it.

## The essence of a case statement

Let's go over the basic components again. To put it as simply as I can, a case statement must be brief, state its objectives, verify the need for them, and show what reaching them will mean to the organization, the community, and the prospect. To achieve this it should include a

- brief history of your organization, including its philosophy and mission,
- description of what your organization does or provides,
- view of your organization's current capabilities and future plans and their impact on the organization or the community,
- listing or description of your campaign and organizational leadership, such as faculty, staff, administration, advisory committees, and trustees,
- breakdown of opportunities for supporting the cause including specific levels of gifts for major needs, and
- information on the kinds of gifts that can be made (cash, bequests, stock, real property, etc.) and how to go about making a gift or getting in touch with persons who can assist in this.

Include up-to-date names, addresses, and phone numbers and display them prominently.

Finally, if you're producing a printed piece, the case statement should be easy and pleasant to read, attractive to the eye with interesting photos or art work, and always leave the reader wanting more. In length, use no more copy than will fit on ten to fifteen double-spaced pages to tell your story and take up no more than a third of the space with copy. Use good art work, fresh new photographs, lively, informative captions, and well-placed "callouts," headlines, and charts and graphs to underscore your theme. The look should be contemporary, but not gimmicky or glitzy. "Understated elegance" is an oft-used phrase that applies to most institutional pieces, but one size doesn't fit all. Your organization's character, mission, budget, and constituency should determine the size, cost, and appearance of your printed statement.

## The campaign plan

This is the road map for your campaign. How you're going to get there from here. It's usually written a year-and-a-half or even two years before your kick-off date, and its primary purpose is to let all key parties know what is expected of them and when. Ideally, the campaign plan is a marriage of a strategic plan drawn up by the chief officers or trustees of your nonprofit organization and a fund-raising plan, based on the development savvy of your chief fund raisers, be they employees or consultants. The strategic plan should identify strengths and weaknesses, lay out where the organization needs to go in the future, and state what needs to be strengthened, trimmed, or added. Its view is broad and takes in the competition and the general field of play. It will list specific needs, goals, and aims (including price tags), for moving forward. The fund-raising plan tells management what part of the strategic plan can be met by the development people, how long it will probably take, and what they think is the best way to do it. It is the tactical arm of the campaign.

A typical campaign plan, then, will include the following items, give or take a few variations:
- **An introduction** which sets forth the reasons for having a major campaign;
- **The basic premise**s or conditions of the campaign including that the nucleus fund will be large enough, that key donors will respond, that gifts will be sought in all forms and from all sources, etc.;

- **An explanation of how you arrived at your campaign goals** and the potential for reaching them;
- **The main areas of focus** within the general goals;
- **The significance** of the nucleus fund to success;
- **A timeline** showing what must happen at all key stages of the campaign;
- **What types of gifts** you will and won't count towards the goal;
- **The nature and role of the campaign leadership**, including volunteers and professional fund raisers;
- **Your constituencie**s, including where you expect the money to come from, and the number of major prospects;
- **Who will do the major gift solicitations;**
- **A communications plan**, including the campaign logo, mission and case statements, and marketing and public relations efforts over the length of the campaign;
- **A gift receipting** and stewardship plan;
- **Staffing, space, equipment, and other budget needs;**
- **A conclusion** summing up why the campaign is worth the investment of people, time, and effort and what it will mean to the future of the organization; and
- **Appendical material**—including charts, graphs, and survey information that reinforce the views expressed in the plan.

Clearly there is a lot of work involved here, yet your campaign plan need not be overly detailed or long. Just say exactly what must be done, when will be the best time to do it, and who will be expected to do what when that time comes. Since it is an internal document, only a few copies will be needed and these can be typewritten, double-spaced, photocopied versions which are easily annotated and altered. If all goes well, your plan should invite both written comment and discussion from key leaders in your campaign. When this happens, you will know that they have "bought in" to your ideas and are excited about the campaign's potential. The worst response you can get to your campaign plan is silence.

# Position papers

A position paper is a cross between a proposal and a letter of inquiry. You're not exactly asking the prospect for money, but you are feeling them out in detail about the idea and seeing if they might be interested in discussing things a step farther. Sometimes the request for a position paper comes from the prospect. Some people call them "conversation memos." What the position paper or the conversation memo does is say, "Look, such-and-so presents a real problem (or opportunity). This is where we stand on the issue, these are our qualifications, and this is what we've invested to address the problem. We believe that this is where you stand on the question. If this is so, shouldn't we get together?"

Position papers can save a lot of unnecessary work and frustration and make an excellent way to follow up a telephone inquiry. ("Let me send you something on paper and then we can talk about it some more.") They keep the door open for submitting a formal proposal and can often lead to insightful comments and remarks from the prospect in subsequent letters or conversations. They serve as a useful tool for defining your position to your own leadership and board members and assuring that everyone is on the same wavelength. (Sometimes the value in the exercise of drawing up a position paper is discovering that your nonprofit agency really isn't geared to dealing with the issue at hand as well as you thought it was. Consequently, it raises the further question as to what you should do to correct the problem.)

These papers should be short. From one to three single-spaced pages. They should also be broken up by informative headings and subheadings. Use "bullets" to highlight key points. It's a good idea to draw up position papers for each of the key programs in your campaign plan. That way, one will always be at hand to use when needed and they can be quickly updated rather then written from scratch for each occasion. I once wrote ten different position papers in a single week while I was at the University of Pennsylvania, each for a different aspect of the Wharton School's programs. A lot of work for one week, but they served admirably all through a five-year campaign, being used not only for discussions, but as resource material for letters, phone calls, and personal visits.

## Check list

- ☐ Does your mission statement clearly define your organization's basic philosophy, purpose, and goals? Is it up to date or does it need changing? Does it sound stuffy?
- ☐ Does your case statement set your organization apart from the competition?
- ☐ Does your case statement present your institution's vision of the future and outline its plans in a way that is easy to read and remember?
- ☐ Will the reader understand *what* you want him or her to do, *when*, and *why?*

- [ ] Have you indicated where the funding will go with price tags attached for each component?
- [ ] Does your case sound positive, optimistic, and upbeat about the future?
- [ ] Does your case include your organization's history and track record?
- [ ] Have you accurately described your campaign and organizational leadership?
- [ ] Is there a list of gift opportunities?
- [ ] Have you explained how to make a gift and where to send it?
- [ ] If your case statement is printed, does it look contemporary without looking expensive?
- [ ] Does your campaign plan set forth the reasons for the campaign and explain how you arrived at your goals?
- [ ] Have you shown what your campaign will focus on?
- [ ] Is there a timeline showing what needs to happen at various stages of the campaign?
- [ ] Have you spelled out the role of campaign leaders?
- [ ] Have you shown where the money must come from to succeed?
- [ ] Did you include a communications, marketing, and stewardship plan?
- [ ] Have you spelled out what running the campaign will cost in terms of new staff, space, and equipment?
- [ ] Does your campaign plan end on a high note about what the campaign will mean to the organization and everyone involved?
- [ ] Is your position paper three single-spaced pages or less?
- [ ] Is it broken up into key components by subheads or "bullets"?
- [ ] Does it spell out your organization's position on the question in a way that invites further discussion?

## *Exercises*

- Find out what local organizations are having a capital campaign and get a copy of their case statements. Try to get at least five or six. Which one seems best to you? Why? Which seems weakest?
- Find out who wrote the case statement you liked best and ask to interview them. Learn all you can about the planning, cost, and distribution of the document. Save your notes and write a short newspaper or magazine article about how and why these things are produced. See if you can sell it or get it published in a fundraising journal. How much did you learn about case statements

from this process?

- Collect and study at least six mission statements from six different types of charitable organizations or agencies. How many have the three main points of "character," "philosophy," and "reason for being?" How many points do they have in common? Which is the clearest and most effective?
- Draft a mission or case statement for an organization you belong to or are familiar with. Does it capture the essence and spirit of this group?
- Try to secure a copy of at least one campaign plan to study. You'll probably need a friend who works in development to help you with this. (They are not meant for the public eye for reasons of privacy and donor protection.)

# Chapter Eight

# Using the New Visual and Audio Media

**T**RADITIONAL fund raising has always depended heavily on the printed word. Until the early sixties, it was the medium Americans were used to for conveying and receiving important information. Newspapers were more influential than television and magazines more influential than newspapers. Books reigned supreme as educational tools. But that's exactly when things started to change. With the advent of color television, we became more image oriented and the advertising dollar abandoned the print media. Magazines such as *Life* and *Look* were "history," as they say today. By the seventies, cable television had gotten a toehold. By the late eighties electronic communications had exploded. Video recorders and cameras, desktop computers, laser printers, color copiers, Fax machines, voice mail, and multimedia programs were available to just about anyone. Suddenly, it was possible to write and produce a complete video production within a single shop, putting new marketing and advertising tools within range of all but the smallest budget. Radio stations, which had stolen the play from print media for a few decades, fell into third place, becoming a specialty medium. We are now dealing with a visually oriented generation that reads not less, but differently, and has an extremely short attention span. Even learning has become a fragmented experience because young professors in our universities are themselves children of the electronic age in communications. Blame it on Disney. He started it all.

Properly handled, visual media have great immediacy and emotional appeal. Real places, real people, real voices combine in powerful and impredictable fashion to involve the audience in your message: Falling leaves on a hazy autumn afternoon, a child's face in a hospital clinic, or the joyful sound of an oratorio touch people in places not easily reached otherwise.

But does the medium get the message across, or is it, as Marshall McLuhan said, the message itself? If you are thinking about using something other than traditional fund-raising communications tools, you'll need to know a little bit about what you're doing, what the implications are, and who you should be dealing with. Be sure you're buying the steak and not just the sizzle. In my view, although a good slide show, video, or documentary film can be extremely useful, they don't have the staying power and versatility of the written word. Nor do they deliver as much bang for the buck. At best, they complement, but do not yet replace the written word. I say "yet" because what's coming in multimedia communications is unprecedented in the human experience. Optical cables, satellite transmissions, holography, and superfast computers will make future presentations of all kinds instantaneous, three-dimensional, and instantly malleable. Image manipulation, voice simulation, and data massaging hold forth scary possibilities. Truth, never a clear or permanent concept to begin with, will be decided by whoever sits at the central control panel linking satellites, telephone systems, and computer and TV networks. The big problem with this magical "brave new world" which Shakespeare foresaw in *The Tempest*, is that not everyone will have access to it for a long time to come. But even when they do, someone will still have to sit down and write the plot for what they will hear and see.

Let's examine some options you may be tempted with in the future and what their pluses and minuses are. Keep in mind, however, that my specialty is writing. What I have to say here about other media should be taken as guidelines of a general kind. Consider them accordingly.

## Picking the best medium for the job

The differences between electronic media and print media are fundamental and easy to grasp.
- Electronic media such as television and radio, reach out to a large, but unknown audience at relatively high cost *per eventual donor.* They are all but incapable of "closing the deal." That is, getting someone to actually send you a gift of any real impact.

Eventually someone has to send a letter, make a phone call, or pay a visit. People who know the game, for example, will tell you that all those TV evangelists and "self-help" experts are less interested in your first-time donation or sale, than getting your address and phone number to build up their direct mail lists and telemarketing data banks.

- Print media, particularly direct mail appeals, are highly focused, reaching out to audiences already partially or wholly attuned to your organization's views and aims. If they do not actually result in a gift, they almost invariably pave the way for one.

So that's the difference. Electronic media usually mean big-ticket price with low potential return. Print media mean a smaller investment with a higher potential rate of return.

What should you pick? The answer depends on what are you trying to accomplish, how soon, and for whom. And let's not forget the most important question. What's the trade-off? What are you giving up (or gaining) in terms of money, time, and effort by choosing one form of communication media over another. Is the risk big or small? Not so easy to decide, and you haven't even had to defend your choice to a committee yet. Maybe that's why virtually every organization, except business corporations with larger budgets, steers clear of the more exotic forms of media to communicate with their public. The people in charge of the purse strings today are more reluctant than ever to authorize expenditures which, in their highly biased view, don't directly affect the bottom line. But these things move in cycles. "Yesterday," slide shows and made-to-order films were hot. Every executive wanted them. Interactive audiovisual electronic media will be hot "tomorrow." All it takes is one big dog to bark loud about something and all the little dogs start barking too. So maybe it won't hurt to know something about some of these tools, what purpose they serve in fund-raising, and who should do the writing for them.

# Audiovisual Productions

Deep in their heart, everyone wants to write and direct a film, slide show, or a videotape. And why not? It's fun if you are working with the right people. Today's computerized multimedia productions can now combine the virtues of all three techniques, but in most cases, they are still written, produced, and used separately.

### Multiprojector slide shows
These are almost extinct in the fund-raising world today. Their

high production cost, difficulty to transport and set up off-site, and frequent technical breakdown all counsel against this approach. A fourth factor, their tendency to age quickly in a fast-moving society, is another reason to steer clear of them. Such productions work best in special fixed settings such as museums or historical sites. Usually, when a nonprofit's leadership advocates using multimedia slide shows for a campaign or informational purpose, it comes from a person who vaguely remembers seeing something that impressed him or her in the past and was, in fact, probably for an entirely different purpose than fund-raising.

## Single projector slide shows

Thanks to several excellent new computer programs for making slides in-house automatically, the once-mundane single-projector slide show affords an excellent, low-cost opportunity to present important information to committees, board members, and volunteers in a colorful and entertaining style. With the help of a writer with good visual skills, complex facts and numbers can be turned into easy-to-grasp charts, diagrams, and lists. And these shows can be updated in minutes if need be. An added bonus is that once the slide show is on a computer disk, the show can be mailed or transmitted by modem for viewing on a colleague's or prospect's color computer. Animation special effects equal or surpass those of the most expensive multiprojector slide show. Very definitely a tool that's not only here to stay, but is limited only by the skills of the persons using the program.

## Film productions

Film productions require a vast range of skills beyond someone to write the script—cinematographers, editors, lighting designers, directors, and more. Yet they are useful only with large audiences such as for training or orienting large groups of volunteers. Even the excellent campaign films made by United Way every year are seen by a relatively small number of actual donors. Costs aside, I cannot think of a valid reason today for making a film for fund-raising reasons. There are just too many other less-expensive, versatile, and more effective options.

## Video presentations

These highly portable, flexible, and easy-to-make visual tools have the added benefit of being cheap to duplicate and distribute. The universality of TV-VCR units means that if you make a video, it can be viewed by a single individual at home or in the office or hundreds of people in a church hall, community center, or school auditorium. A video can focus on a specific fund-raising purpose or cause, such as a new laboratory; the uses to which annual gifts are put; the shows, plays, and other productions put on by the local theater group; where repairs are needed in the church hall; or the beauties of the arboretum. "Voice-overs" can supply added description and detail, and individual faces, personalities, thoughts, and comments can be captured live. Virtually any element can be changed or moved almost at will, and titles, captions, charts, and diagrams can be dropped in whenever and wherever they are needed. Should the videotape start to look and "feel" dated, sections can be cut out or changed and useful segments can be retained in the updated version.

Some organizations are already using "video case statements" to supplement or supplant the traditional printed case statement. The low cost, versatility, and "user-friendly" quality of contemporary video affords a powerful fund-raising option whose potential is as great (or small) as the imagination and courage of the agency using it.

No matter what form of audiovisual production you choose to support fund-raising activities, you should hire trained professionals to supervise and produce them. Each form, whether it is slides, film, or video, has its own particular idiosyncrasies and grammar. What might be a suitable idea for a the powerful iconography of slides, won't necessarily work with a "hot," interactive communications form like television or the cool detachment and reserve of film. Before you get carried away with the idea of "It will be cheaper if we do it ourselves," talk to and visit the people who do it every day for a living. You will find that the fresh approach, new insights, and tons of experience they have to offer will yield a final product that is far more successful and gratifying than anything you could do on your own.

## Aural and audio presentations

This category includes the use of radio spots, fund-raising telethons, and audio cassettes to get your message across to your audience of prospective donors. Each works in its own way to achieve a specific end.

### Radio

It costs far less to buy time in this medium than it does to buy time on television. This allows you to increase the frequency of your message, which is where its true value comes in. What you want to say and how you choose to say it is entirely up to you. Two things will count toward success. The quality of your script and the professional quality of the voice delivering the message. We're not talking big chunks of time here—20 to 30 seconds is standard. This means you haven't got a word to waste. Imagery should be strong. The language crisp, clear, and as unforgettable as you can write it. How many times have you listened to (or seen) a commercial promoting some business service or product and said to someone else, "What was that all about?" The only purpose of any radio, TV, or print commercial is to sell the product. They are not made to entertain, educate, or enlighten although these are all techniques that can be used effectively. They are made to sell. In the case of fund raising, the message they need to transmit to the hearer is "We need you to help us now." And even the best commercial can do no more than condition or "soften up" the prospect for the ask that will eventually come by a direct mail, telephone, or personal request. You have two choices for recording your radio message. 1) Use the best-quality trained professional male or female voices you can afford, if this is appropriate to the message you are presenting, or, 2) use the natural voices of everyday people by recording and editing "wild" footage. Temple University used a combination of both in its TV and radio messages that link top comedian and alumnus, Bill Cosby, with comments by Temple students. These ads do double duty by encouraging young people to apply to the school and, at the same time, instilling a sense of pride in Temple's graduates. I do not think it a coincidence that financial support for the school increased steadily during the peak use of these devices.

As for timing and distribution, the best time to use radio ads would be just before and during your peak fund-raising period. (They could also be used afterwards to thank all who helped make the drive successful.) Your own demographics of past givers and current prospects (and your organization should have them) will pinpoint exactly where your best potential market is.

Because this is a special tool, try to obtain the services, either voluntary or paid for, of a writer familiar with the techniques and language of this marketplace. The results will be far better that just letting someone "take a shot at it."

### Telethons

A number of sources can tell you how to run an effective telethon—how to find space, pick the best dates, staff it, and organize the calls. But a telethon is only as successful as the people on the calling end of the line. Every caller should be thoroughly rehearsed and armed with a 5" x 7" cards that tell them exactly what to say to potential donors. This material need not be long but the caller should

1. Give his or her name and affiliation with the fund-raising institution.
   ("Hi, Mr. Jones. I'm Mary Smith, a sophomore at Down State U.");
2. Say why he or she is calling.
   ("We're beginning our annual fund campaign this week, and we're hoping that you'll support State again this year."); and
3. State clearly what is wanted.
   ("Last year, you donated $100. We're hoping that you'll join us again this year."
   *or* "Last year you gave $100. Do you think you could double your gift this year?") The caller should then;
4. Explain what the annual gift supports and how important this is.
   ("Did you know that annual gifts are our only source of scholarship funds? Half of all our students need your support.");
   Then they should
5. Ask for the gift.
   ("Can I put you down now for a contribution this year too?").
   Whether the donor says yes or no, the caller should always
6. Thank the person for his or her time and leave the door open for another call.
   ("Gee, that's great. I'll send your reminder and a gift envelope right out. Thanks for helping out." or "Thanks for your time. Would you like me to send you a pledge card in case you change your mind later?").

These six steps—identifying the caller, explaining the purpose of the call, setting up the ask, citing the importance of the gift, asking for the gift, and thanking the prospect and following through—cover all the bases and keep the ball rolling with maximum efficiency.

Generally, the telethon caller will get two kinds of responses: one friendly and one not so friendly. The friendly response will be either positive or negative, in which case there is no real problem. If the prospect is negative, the caller should ask them to think it over. If the prospect is hostile, the caller should end the call as quickly as possible and avoid trying to answer questions or explain situations beyond his or her control ("My son had SAT scores over 1200 and didn't get admitted. Why should I give money to State?"). Having the calling guidelines on paper right in front of them keeps telethon callers focused and helps them get in a higher number of calls per hour.

Obviously, the advice I offer here is bare-bones stuff. Telemarketing, like direct mail, is a highly structured, well-organized activity with rules all its own. If this is your first attempt at the game, get the advice of an experienced telemarketer in setting up your phone campaign.

### Audio cassettes

Here's a chance to bring the "sights" and sounds of your organization to someone far away. The range of what you record is unlimited: the school song (a common favorite) and the crowd at a football game that leads into an appeal to support the athletic program; a mini-drama using local actors that describes your community theater program and sets up the ask; or a soft-sell on the rewards of teaching someone to read that will inspire gifts and recruit new members for your anti-illiteracy program. With the magic of sound effects and background music, an audio tape can have the mental and emotional impact of a much more expensive TV or film presentation.

Add in all the information needed for the hearer to make a gift and you have a point-to-point selling tool that can be extremely engaging. The same production caveats apply here as in the other examples: get professional design and production help. There's a lot of trained talent out there that costs a lot less that you expect. Again, draw on volunteers or students from your local theater groups and drama schools if cost is a problem.

Originality in approach can pay off big in an increasingly competitive environment for the donor's attention and dollars. Making and mailing a high volume of five- to ten-minute audio cassettes from a master tape affords a low-cost compromise between more expensive printed mailings, videotapes, and film. Because people are naturally curious, the element of mystery ensures that audio cassettes will get played. (If you send a brief letter along, don't give away what's on the tape. Just identify the sending organization and tell them "this is something important from _____ that we think you'll be interested to hear.")

Given the universal availability of personal audio cassette players, "boom boxes," and automobile tape decks, this medium represents an underdeveloped and almost unexplored fund-raising opportunity.

The two big questions to ask yourself, as an executive or a writer, in deciding what communications option to use are "Is this what I want my audience to know?" and "Is this the best medium, all things considered, for the job?"

# Check List

☐ Can you use, or should you be using, electronic media to get your fund-raising message across?

☐ Does your slide show have a professional, contemporary look, or is it dated?

☐ Can you produce slides in-house on your computer?

☐ If you are planning a film, is there a cheaper, more effective electronic tool that could be used instead?

☐ Should you have a fund-raising video cassette?

☐ Have you ever explored using radio messages or public-service announcements?

☐ Is your script clear and focused on the primary message?

☐ Are the messages timed to coincide with direct mail or telephone drives?

☐ Have you scripted your telethon and trained the callers before hand?

☐ Does your script close with an ask to give or to increase a gift?

☐ Do your callers know how to handle hostile prospects?

☐ Is your program adaptable for original tape cassette promotion?

## *Exercises*

• Call several local audiovisual production companies and ask them if they do fund-raising productions. Ask if you can visit the studio and see or hear these productions.

• Call the development offices of your local colleges and universities and ask the communications person how he or she uses audiovisual material.

• Keep track of any fund-raising-oriented appeals you see or hear on TV or radio. Are they effective? Why not?

• Visit a service organization that makes computer-generated slide productions. Get a price list or cost schedule.

• Try to find articles on new approaches to audiovisual fund raising in recent issues of *Case Currents* and the *Chronicle of Philanthropy*.

• Check with the station managers at a couple of local radio and TV stations and ask them if any of their public service ads are fund-raising-oriented. Who made them? Try to track down the production company and interview the people on their approach to these pieces.

• Find out how your local NPR or PBS station organizes and runs its telethon. How does the telethon tie in with direct mail?

**Chapter Nine**

# Useful Odds and Ends–
# Citations, Resolutions,
# and Plaques

**M**ANY fund-raising writers cringe when they are asked to write copy for these relatively short and infrequently used stewardship items. They shouldn't. The writer's hesitancy usually stems from general inexperience with citations, resolutions, and plaques, uncertainty about what sort of language to use in writing them, and what significance to accord or assign to the accomplishments and contributions they reflect.

As far as inexperience goes, take comfort from knowing that even if you haven't written many of these things, neither has anyone else. So how you handle it can be largely up to you. As for the language, there are usually three alternatives; you can be stuffy, matter-of-fact, or poetic, depending on whom you are working for and who will receive the award. When it comes to significance, you have to be reasonably honest and careful in what you say. An endowment gift for a new professorship, a library, or a school of medicine would certainly mean more than a small scholarship fund to the same institution. But the sacrifice made by each donor in terms of individual resources may well be equal. And what about acknowledging long years of service to the organization, even though only a few small donations were ever received? That's where each of these instruments serve their purpose in a useful, and generally well-received way.

# Citations

Everyone loves something he or she can hang on the wall or set on the piano that says they are wonderful. Usually 5" by 7" or 8" by 10," these frameable citations can use "canned" copy that's stored in a computer or something that's tailored to the occasion. They can applaud anything from volunteer service to funding an endowed chair. In either case, the copy need not be long. For a major contribution, the citation might have the benefactor's name rendered in calligraphy and should come already framed. Some of the nicer ones I have seen were bound in leather folders instead of framed and sealed with the organization's official seal and ribbon. (You can get gold or red seals at the stationery store and a piece of red or blue silk ribbon just about anywhere.) These citations look more or less like a diploma and are usually presented at luncheon or in a formal ceremony with friends and relatives present. They are always signed by the highest officer of the organization and dated by hand.

In every case, they are deeply appreciated. I have been told (although I don't know because writers are always off scribbling someplace else on such occasions) that men and women have broken into tears when their citation was read aloud. This just goes to show you how much we all need a hug now and then and how few of them we get. I'd say this would constitute reward enough for any writer.

What does such a citation usually contain? Three things mainly:
* A statement expressing the organization's gratitude to the individual or individuals;
* An acknowledgment praising the gift or service rendered; and
* An indication of the significance of this gift or service to the organization's mission and future.

As I said above, the citation should be dated and signed.


# Resolutions

This is the heavy-duty, industrial-sized version of a citation. Often done entirely in calligraphy, it's usually issued by a board of trustees or directors, a faculty, or some similar formal group. The elements and intention are the same as a citation—to provide visible, permanent acknowledgment of some form of contribution. Resolutions, however, tend to be more formal (although they don't have to be) and use such formats as "whereas" to begin each paragraph and "we hereby resolve that, etc.," at the end. The reasons they are bigger are 1) more than one thing needs to be recognized, 2) there is greater personal involvement between the organization and the individual, and

3) this relationship has existed for several years or more.

In the case of major gifts, both resolutions and citations often take the place of or accompany a plaque. Should you need the services of a calligrapher, try your local stationery store, art school, or yellow pages. It's an art form strongly on the rebound and beautiful things are being done these days. If all else fails, call *Calligraphy Review* in Norman, Oklahoma. They'll find someone for you.

## Plaques

Plaques signify acknowledgment of a major gift. More than likely, the gift is a physical facility such as a laboratory, a hospital floor or suite, or a new building or recreational facility. Somewhere there is probably even a parking lot with a plaque on it.

Plaques are easier to do than citations and resolutions, because most of the time the donor will tell you what he or she wants on it. If they don't tell you what they want, be sure you ask them what they want. Whatever you do, always allow the donor to review and comment on the copy for the plaque and its design as well. Show them a paper mock-up before you have it engraved. You'll save a lot of aggravation and money. The writer's problem is translating what the donor wants into something the organization can live with. Sometimes the inscription winds up a simple statement of fact like,

---

**"The Life Sciences Building
was established in 1999
by the XYZ Foundation"**

---

It's best if your plaque inscription is a full grammatical sentence rather than the commonly seen inscriptions that start "In recognition of." In this fashion, the thought is expressed somewhat awkwardly, e.g.,

---

**"In recognition of
the XYZ Foundation's support of
the Life Sciences Building
1999"**

---

My instinct is to say, "What? What's the rest of it?" Not that it really matters much. Plaques, like war memorials, statues, and other public art, are just "there" after a while. For that reason, if you're going to put up a plaque, you may as well give the donors a citation or resolution for their office or den as well.

If you need a better idea of what plaques look like, just visit your nearest hospital or university administration building. The lobby will be full of them.

## Check List

☐ Have you spelled the recipient's name right on your plaque, resolution, or citation?

☐ Have you invited family members and friends to attend the presentation?

☐ Will your "big hitter" say a few words?

☐ Does the citation copy express your gratitude, praise the service rendered, and note its significance?

☐ Have you thought about using a professional calligrapher for major resolutions?

☐ Have you consulted with the donor about the wording, material, and design of your plaque before it goes to the engraver?

☐ Does your plaque copy form a complete and logical statement?

## *Exercises*

- Find out how many people you know have citations or resolutions citing their contributions. Do they display them? What do the documents say? How many do you have? Include awards from professional societies. There will be more than you think. I started collecting mine at the age of ten from the "Vacation Reading Club" at the Philadelphia Public Library. I'm still collecting them.
- Visit a local calligrapher or framing specialist to see how many varieties of citations and resolutions exist.
- Next time you are in or around a public building, school, or hospital, make note of and read the plaques on the walls. They probably cover many years and styles. How old is the oldest one? Which is the most recent? How do they differ?
- Visit a local trophies and awards firm. What percentage of their business comes from plaques? Ask who the biggest customers are.
- Write a citation honoring someone you know for a contribution they have made to the local church, school, or civic association. Expand it into a resolution. See the difference?

# Chapter Ten

# Special Events

**N**o book on fund-raising writing would be complete without a word, at least, on what writing assignments occur in conjunction with the special events that are such a key part of meeting annual fund-raising goals, especially for smaller, community-based organizations. Special events, in fact, so relatively simple on the surface for those who attend them, can be the most complex and difficult fund-raising tasks to bring off well. There are so many things to consider, so many details to check, and so much to do physically as well as mentally in setting up and carrying out alumni dinners, awards banquets, theater nights, walkathons, golf tournaments, holiday receptions, special lectures, and all those other things that keep donors involved and happy.

Good writing can do a lot to insure success. Among the things a writer may be called on to do are

- announcements
- "save-the-date" cards
- reminder notices
- invitations
- follow-up letters
- programs and program notes
- handouts or brochures
- speeches or speaker's notes
- citations
- press releases, and
- thank-you letters to everyone who helped out.

More than you thought, isn't it. And I've probably left out a few things.

The most important element in each of these tasks is *accuracy*. Get the date, facts, and details right and be absolutely certain of the correct spelling and form of all names, places, and titles. The next most important factor is *timing*. Most of these things have to be written well in advance on the event, so they can be reviewed, approved, and ready to go when they are needed. Creativity, always important in arousing interest in the event, takes a back seat to accuracy and timing. It makes no difference how spiffy your invitation is if the date is wrong, the keynote speaker's name has an extra letter or two, and the envelope arrives a week late.

The steps involved in carrying out most of the writing assignments listed above, such as letters, speeches, citations, and press releases have already been covered or will be covered elsewhere in this book, and samples of other items, such as invitations, programs, and save-the-date cards are relatively easy to obtain. I will limit my comments, then, to five basic items, a few general remarks about planning special events, and some methods and resources that will help yours succeed.

## Save-the-date cards

Usually the first step in informing donors and prospects about your upcoming special event, save-the-date cards are the cheapest way of getting the word out early. They can often be colorful or clever in appearance (shaped like the head of an oversized golf club or theater ticket, for instance). But these cards should never overreach themselves. Don't try to get more information on them than you need. And keep it simple. For example,

### It's tee-up time!
April 1 at the Osage Country Club.
The Third Annual Alumni Celebrity Golf Outing to benefit the Franklin U. Endowment Fund.
Circle your calendar now!
Call 123-2311 to make your reservation.

A short headline and the classic "who, what, when, where, why, and how" are all you need to send a perfect save-the-date card.

## Invitations

The wording and appearance of an invitation should complement the nature of the special event and the organization sponsoring it. It should also take into consideration the nature of the audience it addresses. The invitation might be as formal as one for a wedding or commencement invitation or as casual and contemporary as an announcement for the new neighborhood fitness club. Whatever form it takes, an invitation should make it clear as to

1. Who is extending the invitation
   (The president of Benjamin Franklin University...)
2. What the nature of the event is
   (The Franklin Society Annual Recognition Dinner)
3. Where and When it is being held
   (The Downtown Club, 7 P.M., Friday, June 13...)
4. Why it is being held
   (to honor major donors, etc.)

The invitation can also mention such things as valet parking or cocktails at six, if appropriate. The response device, which is mailed along with the invitation, can, and probably should, repeat information included on the invitation along with an RSVP deadline, space for the name, address, and phone number of the invited parties, and the usual check-off places for "will/will not attend."

A self-addressed (but not stamped) return envelope should also be included.

Simple steps really, but you would be astonished at what people forget or leave out of this package so essential to your special event's turnout.

Invitations to less-formal gatherings can be sent in letter form, but the same basic rules apply regarding what information should be included. Frequently, the only response device in these informal invitations is a phone number listed in the last paragraph of the letter. Obviously, the very nature of a letter invitation conveys an entirely different kind of message to recipients. And, sometimes, that's exactly what you want.

## Programs

You can put just about anything you wish in the program except the menu. That should be a separate item.

Try to make use of every page.
- The cover design should include the name, date, and place of the event.

- The agenda page or pages should present, in order, the names and titles of persons offering words of greeting, invocations, or introductory remarks. Persons presenting and receiving awards, or making announcements, speeches, and closing remarks should also be listed in order of appearance.
- Biographical material about the key speaker is always useful. It should be short and clear and be on its own page. You should be more interested in capturing character here than providing a laundry list of past appointments and educational credentials.
- Historical background or information about the campaign, organization, or institution should be similarly presented. Don't assume that because they may already know who you are or why they are here that they don't care about this information. They do.
- A page or two should be set aside to list and acknowledge major donors or volunteers.
- The last page should never be blank. Always use it to convey a brief visual or written message about your organization, even if it is only your logo, motto, or name and founding date.

## Timetables and Checklists

People running one-person shops, or those still unfamiliar with the hectic nature of planning and running special events, should keep in mind that writing tasks are just the tip of the special-events iceberg; a host of other considerations are involved. To keep track of such things, most special events professionals arm themselves with timetables and checklists that allow them to keep step-by-step and day-by-day track of what has been taken care of and what still needs to be done. Timetables, which focus on such things as ordering printed material, food service, transportation, entertainment, publicity, and space reservations, start well in advance, usually eight weeks or more, and gradually work their way down to four weeks, two weeks, the week before, the day before, the day, and the day after the event.

Among the many tangible and intangible problems to consider are the objective of the special event, the nature and character of the audience, the place it will be held, and the type of event. Is a celebrity involved and what headaches might that entail (security, accommodations, escape clauses, etc.)? Important, too, are the number of people coming, the time of year, the space being used, temperatures (every 50 people raise it 3°), ambient noise, the availability and quality of audiovisual and audio equipment, lines of sight, seating plans, housekeeping, photographers, travel time to and from the site, parking, rest rooms, stairs, elevators, and access and facilities for the physically challenged.

Awesome, isn't it?

To help you cope with this overwhelming range and variety of detail, tools ranging from a meeting planner's "slide rule" to books of etiquette and preprinted timetables and checklists are available. For information on where to secure them, call or write:

Meeting Professionals International
1950 Stemmons Freeway
Suite 5018
Dallas, TX 75207-3109
(214) 712-7700

*or*

International Special Events Society
1500 Market Street, 12th Floor
Philadelphia, PA 19102
(215) 387-8780

These organizations will put you in touch with your local special events professional groups and supply other information you will find invaluable.

## Check list

☐ How many written items will you need for your special event? Make a list.

☐ What will you need first, second, third, etc.?

☐ Have you checked correct spellings of all names, titles, places, etc.?

☐ Do you know all you should about the people who are coming?

☐ Does your program make use of every page?

☐ Have you made timetables and checklists for each stage of planning?

☐ Did you scout out the site thoroughly for potential problems?

☐ Did you thank all who helped make the event a success?

## *Exercises*

- Call the special events office at a nearby college or university and ask them for samples of written or printed materials they have used over the past three years.

- Look up articles on special events management in such sources as *Case Currents, The Chronicle of Higher Education*, and *Fund Raising Management*. How much do they talk about writing?
- Volunteer to handle special events publicity and marketing at a church, school, or nonprofit social service agency in your community.
- Talk to graphic designers and direct mail writers about some of their special-events projects or experiences.
- Look at some special events promotions you have gotten and re-do them in what you consider a more effective or more creative way.

# Chapter Eleven

# Public Relations and Press Releases

**P**UBLIC relations is a field unto itself. It has changed tremendously in the last decade, becoming more market-driven than service-oriented. Supporting fields, such as demographics and computer-based electronic communications, have helped to make such old stereotypes as the publicity "flak" who threw whatever he or she could against the media wall in the hopes that some of it would stick a thing of the past. Public relations, which used to rely on schmoozing and the three-martini lunch, is a much more precise and focused profession today. And we're all the better for it.

The debate about how much of a role public relations and marketing should play in any development effort still rages. You can get a convincing argument supporting their claim for holding the dominant position from all three sides. At some organizations, the development office is subordinate to the marketing department (a relationship I dislike); at others development runs the PR department and the marketing function barely gets a nod; at still others, each office retains its independence, doing what it does best and playing a voluntary supportive role for each of the other groups. Except for empire builders, most people find this the most satisfying and successful arrangement.

Let me give you an example of what can happen when power isn't shared. Suppose the marketing department is top dog at a major hospital. It decides to push the cardiology department this year and insists that the PR and development offices follow suit. What may happen is that the PR office is trying to peddle heart-related stories of no interest to the press and ignoring some really good genetic research being done by the molecular biology people. The development office, too, is off plugging grant proposals for clinical cardiology care which have no chance of succeeding. Bottom line at the end of the year? Cardiology patient volume goes up a tad, the news media get steamed at the PR people for not cooperating enough on other stories or inquiries, and the development director gets canned for not meeting overall goals. A extreme example, perhaps, but it does happen when agenda get out of whack.

Whatever situation you may find yourself in, the development writer or communications person usually does not deal directly with the media. The exception, of course, is the small or one-person shop. In this capacity, especially in the middle of a campaign or upon the receipt of a major gift, you may quickly become the point person for questions from local newspaper, radio, and TV reporters and editors interested in what's going on. This is where the research, preparation, and writing that goes into a good press release will serve you well. If you do your job right, coming up with the answers reporters want will be easy. For the sake of argument, this chapter addresses, however briefly, the basic problems faced by a one-person, many-hats development office in preparing and distributing a press release.

## Keeping the recipient happy

There are two kinds of press releases. One that you send to the print media and one that you send to the electronic media. Neither side wants to get the other version by mistake.

The print media release resembles a traditional news story, one that presents information in a way that builds on and amplifies each element. These are relatively easy to do, and we will discuss the nuts and bolts involved in a minute.

The radio or TV release is different. Here you need an ultra-condensed version of the basic release written in ultra-simple language. It should be double- or triple-spaced, use small words and short sentences, and be readable in easy-to-say "sound bites" of ten or fifteen seconds. Most TV and radio stations won't bother to rewrite a print media release if they have another story they can use in its place. It's wise, then, to take the small trouble to do two, or even three versions: one each for newspapers, TV, *and* radio.

If you have a visual, such as a color photo, slide, or graphic to send to the TV station along with the copy, so much the better. Many organizations send a video tape along with their releases today. What I am saying, in effect, is that the closer you come to doing the station's work for it, the better luck you'll have getting "space" on the air. To be effective for radio stations, your press release language should have strong visual connotations if you can work them in naturally. For example, you might say that "Thanks to a $5 million gift, a bright green stretch of natural grass replaced the scruffy artificial turf at Franklin Stadium today...etc."

Before you send a press release out to the electronic media, read it aloud and change words or structures that will confuse the hearer or cause a news reader to stumble. And make sure that the brief information gets all of your message across. Then ask a disinterested party if your copy sounds easy to listen to and follow.

## The basic release

Press releases serve two purposes. One is informational; the other is political. Knowing that you are reaching out to the media in a professional way keeps management and donors happy. No matter how much they groan about it, everyone likes to see his or her name in the paper in a favorable context. Another political aspect of press releases is that they tell the media that your organization is a "player." Even if they don't use a particular story, it keeps you in their eye. Don't ever discount the value of that.

The format of a release is simple. First of all, *it should go on your organization's letterhead or standard, preprinted press release form bearing your organization's logo and name.* A little creative thinking can make your release stand out from the crowd. Years ago, when I was at the University of Pennsylvania News Bureau, we ran a red and blue strip along the left-hand side of the first release page so editors could spot it easily when looking through filed-away pieces. (The best news writers often keep files of interesting releases as they piece together a future story.)

Okay. What else does your release need?

Put *the date you send it out* at the top right or left.

Next put the phrase *"For immediate release"* under the date. Don't fool around with future release dates. It annoys people. Either release the story or don't send it out. If it's hot stuff, someone always jumps the release date anyway.

Under or opposite the "immediate release" phrase put *the name and phone numbers of people who should be called in regard to the story. Include the area code* even if your immediate distribution is local. If the Associated Press picks the story up, you may eventually need to send the release to people out of town or out of state.

*Write a headline that summarizes the story.* For example "Benjamin Franklin University Gets $10 million Gift for New Sports Medicine Center." No need to be tricky. Just tell them what happened.

*Have a good lead sentence.* Tell them something special regarding the nature of the grant, such as: "Injured BFU athletes will no longer have to travel long distances for special care," or "A man who never held a job in his life has just given BFU $10 million." Now that *would* be a story. Usually the lead sentence will be tied in with the identity or purpose of the donor. Perhaps he or she is a grad who became a famous athlete whose career was saved by a BFU doctor. That sort of thing. Use what's there, and it will be interesting enough.

After that just do the standard who, what, when, where, why, and how treatment. Keep the paragraphs short and keep the release to one page or maybe a page and a half. You don't want to tell the media everything. If they are interested, they'll want to dig a little and put their own brand on the piece. If there is a truly special aspect to the story, you may want to include a separate piece to accompany the story. In this case, it could be a fuller background on the donor with a picture or the latest scoop on advances in high-tech sports medicine. Use stuff that will not only help the reporter but whet his or her appetite too.

When you get to the end of the story, just put three "#"s or a series of dashes in the center of the page. Only real old-time reporters put -30- at the end anymore.

## Know the media

To get a good response, it's important that you know your local press and electronic media people or have access to someone who does. This saves time and gets your message to the place and persons who will find in it fodder for their own purposes. This sounds cynical, but the more good your information will do the newsperson, the more likely you will get good coverage. Even common sense tells you not to call the sports desk with a story about a science grant unless that story is about a gift for a new sports medicine center. If you know what reporters and editors are looking for in general through conversations you have had with them or from stories that seem to be much in the news, you'll know which hot button to push. That's why, if you are lucky enough to have one, your PR office will always have a better sense of who to call and where to place material.

# Sending out the news

I doubt whether you will ever have to hold a press conference. The last time I did, it involved a Nobel Prize. If you do though, be sure to find a good place to have it, make sure all your key people will be there, and tell them to speak for the record when answering questions. After all, you called this thing, so don't play games with the reporters. Have a good press kit ready too, including all forms of the release, biographies, and any photo art you have. Simple pocket folders in bright colors can be picked up in volume at any stationery store to hold this material.

Most of the time, though, you'll just be mailing or faxing the material to your media targets. If there is really a rush, or you want to be sure it gets there, hand-deliver the stuff to special news outlets. Even if it means getting on the bus and going to the big city. Sometimes release information can be sent on-line over computers. *Call key people before you send them your release so they'll be looking for it to arrive.* You may even trigger a story by the call alone. Then call them back the next day and ask if they have the material yet and if there is anything else you can do for them.

If you don't know where to send your release, there are many good media guides you can use to look up names, addresses, job titles, and phone numbers of media people in your area. Try the following sources:

> Gale Directory of Publications and Broadcast Media
> Gale Research Inc.
> Detroit-Washington, D.C.-London
>
> Burrelle's Media Directories
> Livingston, N.Y.

For more detailed advice on publicity and press releases, your local library probably has these and other books you can use.

A final word of advice. Don't be intimidated by media people. They need story ideas just as badly as you need publicity. If you follow the basic steps outlined here, you'll do fine.

# Checklist

☐ Have you identified your best media targets?
☐ Did you make radio and TV formats of your basic release? Did you read them aloud?

☐ Did you send a visual along?
☐ Does your release format contain the key elements it needs: release date, names and phone numbers, a headline, etc.?
☐ Did you make advance phone calls to the media?
☐ Did you make follow-up calls after sending them the release?

## *Exercises*

- Call several local university or corporate public relations offi-cers and ask for sample copies of news releases and press kits they have sent out lately. They'll have plenty of left-overs.
- Ask these persons about how they distribute their releases now. Do they fax them, use computers, or have other special techniques?
- Look through media directories for information about newspa-pers, magazines, and radio and TV stations in your area. Put a list together of those media persons you think might use materi-al you send them in the future. Call two or three to get acquainted.
- Get in touch with the local public relations society and ask them for a membership directory. Ask if you can attend their meet-ings or be added to their mailing list.
- Take a course in public relations at your local community college.
- Add a few recent books on contemporary public relations prac-tice to your professional library.
- Have lunch with a local PR professional. They do it well.

**Chapter Twelve**

# Speeches

**T**HE fund-raising writer is often called on to write speeches for events related to fund-raising. Usually they are not long, and, for the most part, are quite specific in what they deal with. For example, the dedication of a building or a facility, the opening of a special alumni drive, or an appeal to a particular segment of your constituency, such as the neighborhood business group, Rotarians, or Lion's Club. These can be productive and useful occasions, not only for securing gifts, but for lining up new volunteers or getting leads on hot prospects. That's why *any* speech you write should be interesting, provocative, and memorable. At least for an hour or two afterwards.

The problem is, many presenters have terrible public speaking skills. Most of us, in fact, have terrible speaking habits in general. Anytime we have to make a comment more than a few sentences long, we're forever getting stuck and saying "You know" or "Uh uh er uh" over and over. Most of us don't know when to shut up and listen either. We're always interrupting the other person's thought. (You can do that in a speech, too, if you don't pause often enough to allow the audience time for your key thoughts to sink in.)

Lucky the speech writer who is working with an experienced and cooperative public speaker.

Well, as the writer, there is no way you can correct or prevent bad habits in your client, but you can control the content and quality of what he or she is saying. And that is usually enough. More often than not, this is the prime reason for having a development writer do the speech—to keep the organization's speaker on time and target, if you will. (If you happen to be working with a speaker who wishes to write his or her own copy, fine, but make sure you get a chance to look it over. Not to censor it, but to be sure it covers all the fund-raising points it should.)

Speech making is a lost art today. We live in the age of sound bites. Instead of the rule being "Inspire your audience" it has become, "For Pete's sake, don't offend anyone." Hence, the insipidness of modern public oratory. Today, in a nation that knows nothing of politics, everything has become political. I feel this is somewhat of a tragedy. The great speeches of American history, now a permanent part of our literature and heritage, are all those of someone willing to take a position, let the chips fall where they may.

## A model to emulate

Who can forget Martin Luther King's stirring "I have a dream" speech in the 1963 civil rights march on Washington:

"I have a dream that one day on the red hills of Georgia the sons of former slaves and the sons of former slave owners will be able to sit down together at the table of brotherhood..."

And its ringing conclusion.

"This will be the day when all of God's children will be able to sing with new meaning, 'My country 'tis of thee, sweet land of liberty, of thee I sing...When we let freedom ring, when we let it ring from every village and every hamlet, from every state and every city, we will be able to speed up that day when all of God's children, black men and white men, Jews and Gentiles, Protestants and Catholics, will be able to join hands and sing in the words of the old Negro spiritual, 'Free at last! Free at last! Thank God almighty, we are free at last.'"

You can hear the living voice, can't you?

Aside from Dr. King's brilliant delivery, what made this speech work so well? For one thing, the speech's language was simple, and its message was delivered in the context of familiar experiences and ideas. Cashing a bad check. Blowing off steam. Getting out of jail.

For another, it was a speech rich in contrasts, analogy, and imagery. ("...a joyous daybreak to end the long night of captivity," "...from the quicksands of injustice to the solid rock of racial brotherhood." It drew on biblical, Shakespearean, and historical sources. (The "valley of segregation,...This sweltering summer of the Negro's legitimate discontent,...When the architects of our republic wrote the magnificent words of the Constitution and the Declaration of Independence...") It was full of passion and honesty. It rang with music and poetry. It reiterated and summed up the major points. It was full of urgency. As it spelled out the goals of the civil rights movement, it built from thought to thought to an irresistible and unforgettable conclusion—we will be free and equal now! Most important of all, it was a speech that people felt comfortable listening to. It wasn't intimidating, pedantic, or dull. It was well paced. It appealed to both the emotions and the intellect. Such a speech is virtually a model for all speeches and well worth studying.

## There's more to speech making than talking

If rousing oratory seems to be a thing of the past, public speaking skills are still useful whether you're addressing a small group of business or government executives, an alumni meeting, or a professional organization. Anyone who is called on to address an audience should take the time to learn something about the vocal and dramatic skills required and what unspoken signals body language communicates to the audience. Did you know, for instance, that such simple things as raising your eyebrows, shrugging, or opening your arms at your side will make an audience more receptive to your ideas? How significant is eye contact? Very. But that's another side of the coin and one we're not dealing with here. We want to talk about some of the fundamentals of putting an interesting talk together.

Speech writing is still an important craft, and it can be a stimulating intellectual challenge that is a joy to do. If you have good information, good ideas on how to present it, and sound basic speech organization, you're on your way to writing a successful piece. The broader your interests and the wider your experience, the better job you will do. History, politics, literature, science, medicine, language, and the lively and fine arts all come into play when you are writing a speech. And the deeper the well, the sweeter the water.

President Franklin D. Roosevelt once advised a son that the best way to make a speech was to "be brief, be clear, and be seated." But there's a bit more to it than that. In one chapter, I can't possibly cover all the things you need to know to be at the top of your form, but I can get you started. After that, there are some wonderful, well-written, and fascinating books that will help you hone your skills. I will list them for you later.

## Things you need to know

Let's get started. You've just been told by the boss that you need to write a speech for the chairman of the board who is going to address a meeting of financial analysts on the subject of your organization's upcoming capital campaign. What do you do first? After the panic subsides, that is.

First of all, ask yourself some simple questions:

• What do I know about the speaker?
• What do I know about the audience?
• What do I know about the subject?
• How long a speech do they want?

Chances are you already know a great deal about the subject, so you can put that issue on the back burner for now. And you probably have a file on the speaker that you can augment with a few phone calls and perhaps a personal interview. The writer and the speaker should get together to kick around a few ideas and get a feel for each other's style. Unfortunately, this is the exception rather than the rule. Always try to get a meeting or two, and have all your questions set up in priority order in case you run out of time. At least you'll have background on the major issues. Be cordial, but never waste a busy person's time. You can always call back.

The audience is the central factor. After all, they are the reason you will be writing this speech in the first place. Finding out all you can about the audience is vital to enabling the speaker to establish a rapport with them right off the bat. Who are they? What interests do they have in common with your organization? What things about your organization and its goals would interest them most? You're looking for "hot buttons" that will let you frame a sound speech in the context of the hopes, aspirations, and emotional needs of the audience. You've got to turn them on and keep them on. And one thing in your favor, and that you should make use of as both a writer and a speaker, is that they really do want to be a good audience. They want you to tell them things that they need and want to know. They want you to be wise and witty. They want to like you. It's your job as the writer to close that gap between speaker and audience by winning them over with words.

What do we need next? How about a theme? Subject and theme are not the same thing. If the subject is the campaign, for example, the theme will probably be why the campaign is important to them, their community, and their business activities. Defining the theme will help you gain focus and almost automatically organize and structure your thinking.

Now we need a title. A title should never be a throwaway effort. It is the first thing your potential audience will see and make a judgment call on. "Do I want to spend my time on this?" is what they will ask themselves. If it's not catchy, they aren't coming. At least not as many as you would wish. Something in the title should immediately arouse their personal interest.

## The three parts of a speech

This brings us to the next three items: the opening of the speech, the middle of the speech, and the conclusion of the speech. And by conclusion, I mean in the true sense of the word—to arrive at by reasoning (from the Latin "concludere," to shut up or enclose), not merely to come to an end. These three elements all play off and reinforce one another.

### The opening

Your speech's opening lines should immediately engage the interest of the audience in the speaker as a person and identify that speaker as a man or woman much like themselves. It might start with something as innocuous as an anecdote about getting the kids off to school after the recent snowstorm, the effect of a new tax on the old paycheck, or the standing of the local sports teams. Put them at their ease. Bob Hope, a ubiquitous toastmaster, is a master of this form of identifying with the audience right away. From there, you'll want to segue to the three or four, or five key points of the speech outlining what they are about and how they relate to each other and the audience. In other words, you are going to tell them what you are going to tell them, but you are going to do it in a logical way that will allow the listener to easily recall and recapitulate these points later in the speech. This is where such things as alliteration, repetition, and "the rule of three" come so usefully into effect. Even the old saw about speeches reflects the rule of three. "Tell them what you are going to tell them, tell them, then tell them what you've told them." Still good advice if you have no other plan. Alliteration, repetition, and sets of three make it easier for listeners to retain key points and reflect on what else you've said about them during the speech. A classic example is Julius Caesar's "Veni, Vidi, Vici" (I came, I saw, I conquered) which embraces all three principles. A more American "three" might be "Lead, follow, or get the hell out of the way." (That would make an excellent structure for the middle section of a fund-raising speech.) Use parallel constructions, correlative constructions, and antitheses to compare and contrast ideas and images. Abraham Lincoln did. Witness the following examples:

"In giving freedom to the slave, we assure freedom to the free..." (parallel construction)

"I claim not to have controlled events, but confess plainly that events have controlled me." (correlative construction)

"All they ask we could readily grant if we thought slavery right; All we ask they could readily grant if they thought slavery wrong." (antithesis)

At the end of your opening, bridge to the middle section of the speech using a well-thought-out transition so you can elaborate on these core topics. Something like, "Now. Let's examine these issues in detail, starting with my first point. The upswing in the cost of education."

## The middle section

This is where you go into detail on each of the main points. You will probably have subsections listed under each of these headings in your outline. Here, too, is where you will begin to develop the logical arguments supporting your point of view or making your case, including anticipating and answering some potentially opposing views. (Contrariness is part of human nature.) Use any data, quotes, news reports, or ideas that you can dig up to strengthen your hand in building the middle section. But don't draw on other sources too much. Be selective in using such material. A good quote or fact may deserve its own subsection, but don't lose your audience in a forest of facts. Always keep in mind that too many numbers have a numbing effect on human attention. Like a good mystery story, each subsection should hold teasing clues to the speech's conclusion and the vital summing up that occurs there.

When structuring the middle section, don't discount the obvious approach. In his 1941 state of the union speech which came to be known as "The Four Freedoms" speech (see the grouping, theme, and structure right there in the title?), President Franklin Delano Roosevelt described national policy by simply saying "First..., Second..., Third..." and then again later employed strong repetition in endorsing four essential human freedoms:

"The first is freedom of speech and expression—everywhere in the world.

The second is freedom of every person to worship God in his own way—everywhere in the world.

The third is freedom from want...everywhere in the world.

The fourth is freedom from fear...anywhere in the world."
(Note the parallel construction.)

Roosevelt's speech writers, by the way, were a couple of fellows named Harry Hopkins and Robert Sherwood, and they knew a thing or two about both speech writing and people. But in almost all cases,. Roosevelt would take their material and mold it to his own taste and purpose. Which is all a professional speech writer can really hope for or expect. I am always amazed (and embarrassed) when people deliver the words exactly as I have written them. I'd rather they put their own spin on them. No matter what structural scheme you decide on—numerical, alphabetical, categorical, etc., keep it simple. It will make it easier for the speech maker to memorize. Our use of the expressions "in the first place, in the second place," and so forth come from the Roman mnemonic device of assigning different sections of a speech to different rooms in the speaker's house. By imagining themselves in a particular room, they could remember what part of the speech was next. So their structure was architectural and about as simple and familiar as you could wish.

## The conclusion

Now we pull all the previous elements of the speech together and interpret their meaning for audience. Sort of like rounding up all the suspects in the living room and ticking them off one by one until the mystery is solved. Your ending, by the way, should not be easily predictable. Don't let them off the hook too early if you want your audience to maintain interest in what you have to say. Always end on a high note, especially if the subject matter deals with troubling problems or ideas. In summing up, reiterate key points and group them in ways the audience will recall later. Use the alliteration and triads introduced in the beginning. You are working from the general to the specific now. This is not only where you tell them what you told them, but you tell them what you want them to do, how you want them to do it, and when you want them to do it (now). Take a chance here and be inspirational and challenging to them without getting corny or sentimental. Ask them rhetorical questions. "Will you do this for dear old State." "Will you make this sacrifice." "Do you have the courage to take one step forward out of the ranks and volunteer." Be eloquent in a good cause. Do you recall the last lines of Patrick Henry's 1775 speech to the Second Virginia Convention: "Is life so dear, or peace so sweet, as to be purchased at the price of chains and slavery? Forbid it, Almighty God! I know not what course others may take; but as for me, give me liberty or give me death!"

Now that's a challenge.

Fund-raising speech writing doesn't call for anything so powerful or extreme, but the principle is the same. The end of the speech must almost always be on a higher plane than what precedes it. Sometimes quotes can provide us with the eloquence we ourselves do not possess. To honor those who died in the explosion of the space shuttle, "Challenger," in 1986, President Ronald Reagan adapted the first and last lines of a lovely poem about flying written by John Gillespie Magee, Jr., a 19-year-old American who was killed while flying for the Royal Air Force in January 1941: "We will never forget them nor the last time we saw them this morning as they prepared for their journey and waved goodbye and 'slipped the surly bonds of Earth...and touched the face of God.'"

In addition to Dr. King's speech, there are many many other speeches, both real and fictional that you can study to gain an appreciation for fluency and concision of language. Abraham Lincoln's Gettysburg Address is the epitome of concision, wisdom, and human decency. (Garry Wills wrote a masterpiece on it, *Lincoln at Gettysburg*, that should be on every American's— and certainly every speechwriter's—bookshelf.) Susan B. Anthony's 1873 speech on the right of women to vote is a brilliant attack on sexism and the coercion of women and an irrefutable interpretation of the 14th amendment to the Constitution which guarantees civil rights (and implicitly the right to vote) to all persons under the law. General Douglas MacArthur's farewell to the Corps of Cadets at West Point is sheer poetry: "I listen vainly, but with thirsty ear, for the witching melody of faint bugles blowing reveille, of far drums beating the long roll. In my dreams I hear again the crash of guns, the rattle of musketry, the strange, mournful murmur of the battlefield."

Even fiction offers memorable speeches whose structure and language are worth studying. Shakespeare is an excellent source of such speeches, whether they are spoken by villains or heroes. The famous "St. Crispin's Day" speech from *Henry V*, for example, which inspires a worn-out, out-numbered band of English soldiers to fight one last time for king and country, closes on a theme familiar to all of us who write fund-raising material—the benefit of taking part:

This story shall the good man teach his son;
And Crispin Crispian shall ne'er go by,
From this day to the ending of the world,
But we in it shall be remembered –
We few, we happy few, we band of brothers.
For he today that sheds his blood with me
Shall be my brother; be he ne'er so vile,
This day shall gentle his condition;
And gentlemen in England, now abed,
Shall think themselves accurs'd they were not here;
And hold their manhood cheap while any speaks
That fought with us upon St. Crispin's day.

If you think writing speeches is hard, try doing one in iambic pentameter.

## Things to watch out for

### Jargon

Never assume that everyone in the audience is familiar with the buzzwords and acronyms of your subject matter. Physicians, engineers, scientists, and academics are prone to fall back on language they use in every-day transactions. I recall an occasion where a molecular biologist who worked for the federal government was addressing a large of group of university biologists. They understood the science side of what he was talking about but were frequently lost when the bureaucratic terms popped up in the discussion. The speaker had to slow down and back up to clarify individual questions about minor obscurities, which destroyed the pattern of his presentation and made it far less effective.

### Foreign language

Unless you have excellent command of the language you wish to use or quote, shun the use of foreign words and phrases. Sometimes even the way you pronounce a word will give it a different meaning than you intended. This can be embarrassing. One example, which not many people are aware of, is President John F. Kennedy's speech at the Berlin Wall in 1961, "I am a Berliner." While President Kennedy (and most Americans) thought that was what he said, "Ich bin ein Berliner" more closely means something like "I am a jelly doughnut." the correct usage should have been "Ich bin Berliner." The misuse of the article "ein" changed the meaning, but the Germans were so thrilled at the intention of his effort, no one said anything afterwards. President Jimmy Carter had an even worse experience in Poland when what he thought were words of greeting turned out to have a sexual connotation. Foreign languages can wind up a pie in the face.

### Bad jokes

Humor, at the right time and in the right context, can brighten up any speech. Presidents Kennedy and Reagan were masters of the ad lib to dodge an issue or make a point. But humor means different things to different people. The gag you thought was a riot at the Friday night poker game, may not seem so funny to another audience. Far too many jokes have their origins in concealed bigotry, prejudice, and hostile sexual attitudes. It's best to stay clear of even mild forms of home-grown comedy. You only have to think briefly about how many careers were ruined in recent times by casual remarks made in the public media by leading personalities. If you really want to use a gag, pick out something funny Abraham Lincoln, Mark Twain, Dorothy Parker, or Lily Tomlin said. You'll be on safer ground and there are lots of reference books to draw from. A few self-effacing references to comical situations we all find ourselves in from time to time are also okay.

## Timing and scripts

A page of double-spaced speech copy on 8 1/2" x 11" paper will run about 1 to 1 1/2 minutes when spoken.

Margins should be wider than with editorial copy, about 1 1/2" on each side. This makes the material easier to scan. Do not break paragraphs at the bottom of a page. It can cause an awkward pause. Always start and end pages with full paragraphs even if it means leaving a lot of white space at the bottom sometimes.

Do not use dashes. Use standard punctuation. Fragmentary sentences are fine. That's how we speak.

Number pages consecutively.

Center the word "more" on the bottom of each page except the last page, where you will center three number signs (###).

Insert special instructions in parentheses between paragraphs, e.g., ("Pause briefly," "Look at audience; left, right, center," "Point to chart," etc.)

If your speaker prefers to use 5" x 7" note cards, the same rules apply (except for margins), but timing is more difficult. Two or three cards may equal only one 8 1/2" x 11" page. You may have to read the copy aloud and time yourself with a watch. Number every card consecutively with a magic marker in the upper right-hand corner. Use large numbers. That way, if the cards are dropped, and they often are, it will be easy to sort them out again quickly.

Always make sure an extra copy of the speech is at the presentation site. Many speakers leave theirs in the car, office, or home.

## Check list

☐ Do you know the audience the speech is intended for?
☐ Have you discussed the speech's thrust and content with the speaker?
☐ Is your language simple and are the usages and references familiar to the audience. Will they feel comfortable with the speech right away?
☐ Will your speech evoke emotional as well as intellectual reactions?
☐ Does your speech contain all the essential information it should? Is it "solid?"
☐ What is your theme? Can you state it in one sentence?
☐ Is your title intriguing to the audience the speech is aimed at?
☐ Is your speech divided into an opening, middle, and conclusion?
☐ Is there a structural scheme to the speech that groups related ideas and moves it gracefully from point to point?
☐ Have you used the "rule of three," alliteration, and repetition to make it easier for the audience to remember key points?
☐ Will your conclusion seem logical and satisfying to the audience?
☐ Have you avoided using jargon, foreign language, and bad jokes?
☐ Are the pages or cards of the script double-spaced and clearly numbered?
☐ Will an extra copy of the speech be at the presentation site?

## Exercises

- Write a five-minute speech on the value of charitable giving. Put it in the historical context of America's history and traditions. Quote at least two sources, one in the beginning and one at the end. Use the "rule of three" and other devices.
- Read some excerpts from *Vital Speeches of the Day* at your public library. Look for examples of good speech-writing techniques.

- Get the text of a recent presidential speech on a major issue and analyze it point by point. How many characteristics does it have in common with the advice in this chapter? Does it reach the listener as an individual? Does it make its major points effectively? Why?
- Read a book on speech writing.
- Read some of the great speeches of history. Most libraries have anthologies available. Why are these great speeches? Analyze them on paper.

# Chapter Thirteen

# The Value of Good Design

**G**OOD design is something that is with us all the time, although we are rarely conscious of it. The shape, material, and color of the radio you are listening to, the cereal bowl you just stowed in the dishwasher, or the new box of number two pencils you just bought look and feel the way they do because someone sat down and thought about it. You must have liked what the designer came up with, because you paid good money for the final product. Everything, including the lilies of the field, are the result of a design appropriate to that end product and no other. We are surrounded by design, we dwell in the midst of it, and we respond one way to good design and another way to bad.

Written copy, even material not intended for publication in a brochure or a case statement, should look as good as you can make it. This ranges from making sure the draft copy you're sending on to the editorial board or the vice-president for development is free of typos, smudges, and white-out to looking real hard at the quality of the color separations in your new four-color annual report. We live in a visually oriented world, and, just as you look in a mirror before you go out, take a good look at what you are passing on for the judgment of others before it goes out. Don't let a poorly-designed letterhead detract from and even, perhaps, destroy the message of a well-written appeal letter. Good design, as Joseph Moxon pointed out in his *Advice to Compositors* more than 300 years ago, should complement the printed word, not overwhelm it or distract the reader from its message.

Actually, design is even more important than that. Everything you do sends a message about you, your work, and the organization that's paying for your services. What that message is is often up to you. The fund-raising writer frequently doubles as a creative director and contact person for artists, photographers, and graphic designers. In some small shops the writer is the photographer, artist, and graphic designer. But whether you have extensive resources at your disposal or have only minimum input into the design process, there are certain fundamental things you should be aware of.

## The silent critic

First of all, when you are designing a campaign logo, printing a brochure, or producing a new videocassette, remember the "silent critic." All of us carry a silent critic around in our heads. We are forever subconsciously comparing the thing we are looking at to the best of its kind. We don't compare the neighbor's weekend watercolor painting to the one Gramps did; we compare it to Andrew Wyeth or Winslow Homer. We don't compare the way the local high school football team plays to the other local high schools; we compare it to Notre Dame or Penn State. We don't compare the home video about our trip to the zoo to another home video; we compare it to *Jurassic Park*. But we don't know that we do this. We just do. So, given whatever your resources are, always strive to produce the best looking product you can. Remember the silent critic.

There's another side to this principle. Sometimes you hear organizations claim that they are leaders in their field, or among the best. Yet when you look at their communications products, you get another story. Compared to the magazines, brochures, videos, stationery, and other communications material of competitors, theirs looks dated, dull, and second-rate. Boring. Years behind the competition. What they are unwittingly telling their public audience, and we all have one, is "We're not really all that good." (This always happens when noncommunications people have too much to say about design.) If you want to be ranked among the leaders, you have to look the part. Your communications products deliver a powerful visual message about who you are and where you're going. Dress for success.

## The three keys to good publications

To be successful in getting your organization's message across, you need three things: good art, good copy, and good design.

Good art includes high quality illustrations, photographs, charts, diagrams, and typography. (The fonts you and the designer choose are just as important as the way the type appears on the page.)

Illustrations are not much used today because people think they cost too much. In fact, they can often be no more, or even cheaper, than photos. A trained artist skilled in pencil techniques, wash drawings, or pen and ink can turn a routine publication into a thing of beauty. But only if he or she is a trained professional. Don't let anyone foist their cousin's or daughter's work on you because "she can really draw good." Get a pro with a full-ranging portfolio. It costs just as much to reproduce poor work as good, and I have seen good money wasted on true horrors. If you can't afford a pro, try the one of the top seniors at the local college of art. They may be willing to do it for less just for the experience and professional credit. But pay them. Don't try to get art work free.

Good photographers abound, but unless you ask them what they think, many will only shoot what you tell them to shoot. Give the photographer a chance to contribute and use his or her imagination in resolving your problems. Two things I can advise you to do when shooting are:

### Get close to the subject.
The late Robert Capa, one the greatest news photographers who ever lived, said that if the picture didn't turn out right, you weren't close enough. You will be amazed how many pictures turn out better if you get closer. And;

### Shoot faces.
Film director Federico Fellini once said, "Faces! Faces!" to describe his approach to film making. A good rule. Shoot lots of pictures of people doing what they do and prefer your organization's clients to workers and workers to managers.

Closely related to these two thoughts is the "dime rule." Never print a photo, especially a group photo, where the heads shown are smaller than a dime. Such pictures are worthless.

Charts and diagrams can tell a great deal at a glance, but they do it best when done by a professional graphic artist. In one of the nicest bar charts ever made for me, the artist used a drawing of sharpened, oversized, yellow no. 2 pencils of different lengths to represent the bars. (The brochure was a piece for the accounting department of a business school.) The message was instantaneous.

Typography, the arrangement of the type fonts and faces you will choose for printed material, is an art form. Fonts themselves are highly designed entities. Some, like Bodoni or Garamond or Helvetica, are classics that will serve many purposes. Other, more exotic, fonts such as Broadway, have specific, usually limited, applications. A good graphics person knows what to use when.

Copy is also a guide to art and design. If you haven't planted good visual clues in your copy, the artist, the photographer, and the graphic designer are going to struggle to interpret your words. That's why it's so crucial to "think visually" as you write. Good art and design can't save weak copy, they can only make good copy better. There is a book, *Editing by Design*, by Jan V. White, that deals with the mutual influence of copy and page layout.

Good design packages your art and copy in a way that makes it irresistible to the prospect. It says, "Read me. Look at me. Try me out!" We are a people besieged by communicators bidding for our interest and our time. Everyone is tugging at our sleeve and trying to move to the head of the line in gaining our attention. Only a graphic design professional can achieve the results needed to make your piece stand out in a crowd. Do-it-yourself design may save money, but then, you'd save even more money if you didn't produce the piece at all, wouldn't you?

Good art, good copy, good design—the three-legged stool needed to get the most milk out of your communications cow.

## Applying some simple design principles to your printed piece

Whatever it may be that you are producing—a newsletter, a brochure, a case statement—its purpose is to inform and stimulate the reader. It should fascinate and please at the same time. You want your readers to think your outfit is really hot stuff. You want them to like you. You want them to support you. There's no reason you can't reach all of these goals and still have fun being as creative as you like. But beware of designers out to win awards at your expense. Most designers will give you what you need, but every once in a while you will run into a designer that wants to use all the latest gimmicks and fads in the piece he or she is doing for you. That's unnecessary. All artists' roughs and comps begin as simple black-and-white ideas in pencil or magic marker. This is the key. The power is in the original design, not gadget fonts, color photographs, or the slickness of the paper in the final product.

There are two kinds of page layouts that will absolutely lose your reader fast. First is the cluttered page that hurls a dozen different visual signals at the reader. You know what I mean. Four-color art, tilted photos, multiple headlines, six different fonts, captions and "shouts" all over the place that don't seem to connect with anything. The second is a page crammed top and bottom with typography unrelieved by art work, headlines, or captions. Just three or four grey blocks of words from margin to margin.

You don't have to go hog-wild to improve the look of your typed or typeset documents. A few simple rules will help you do that. They are easy to recall, easy to follow, and will save you money too.

### Simplify the typography.

First of all, look at the fonts you are working with. There shouldn't be more than three. One for the body copy, one for headlines and subheads, and one for captions. In many cases, if you use an italic face of the same font, you can get away with two fonts. What about font sizes? Again, try not to use more than three. One size for the main headlines, one size for the subheads, and one size for the body copy and captions. (Caption copy can be either bold or italic to set it off. It should never be the same as body copy.) It's best that the font for body copy and the font for heads contrast. If you have a serif font for the body copy, such as Times, use a sans serif font such as Helvetica or Optima for your headlines and subheads. Serif fonts (the letters have little strokes or hooks on the end of ascending or descending lines) are easier to read in large blocks than sans serif, especially for older eyes.

Whatever font you chose for body copy should be at least 9 or 10 points in size with one point of leading. I wouldn't go larger than 12 points. Subheads can then be 14 to 18 points and heads from 24 to 36 points. It's not a good idea to have too great a size difference among these three design elements. Study your local newspaper for a minute or two. You'll see what I mean.

Some things to look out for. Reversed type (white on black or color) is okay in small doses, but "sparkles" too much for easy reading in large blocks. Stay away from specialty fonts such as Fraktur or Broadway unless you have a specific reason for using them, such as a story tied to Germany or an ad for an alumni trip to see a New York show.

### Simplify the art.

Art can be a number of things, but usually it means a photograph, and more often than not, a black and white photograph. A good guideline to follow (assuming that you have some nice close shots of people doing what they normally do in relation to your organization such as acting in the latest community theater production, distributing food to the homeless, or caring for elderly patients as a hospital volunteer) is to have only one major photo on a page, accompanied by one to three smaller photos of lesser significance. Always have a caption for each photo, even if it's just the person's name or the name of the location. Keep the caption adjacent to the photo, no matter if it's under it, over it, or to the left or right.

If you find that you need to have more than one large photo on a page, maybe the page or pages should be a photo montage. Either the copy or the photos can be dominant, but not both. In most cases, copy will be the central element.

Try not to mix illustrations, particularly clip art, and pie or bar charts with photo art. It's like pickles and ice cream. Charts should get the space and attention they merit because they are there for a specific reason and usually require the reader to stop and study them. Don't reproduce them too small and don't try to pack too much information into any one chart. Clip art or small black-and-white chapbook illustrations (the kind used so beautifully in *The New Yorker*) serve best to break up multiple-page columns of similar copy such as class notes or events schedules.

**Simplify the look.**
Let your copy breathe. Break it up. Strike a balance between how much copy is on the page and how much art.

The first thing to establish is a good ratio of "white space" to type. It's better to add a few pages or cut copy than to push your page's margins and gutters to their extremities. This is true whether you use two, three, or four columns on a page. A column that is too wide (more than two-and-a-half alphabets of the font you're using) or too narrow (words break in strange places) is self-defeating. White space is subjective, more a matter of optical sensibility and spatial relationships than anything you can measure with a ruler or a pica count, but it's easy to see when you don't have enough white space. The page has a constricted look. After you decide how many columns you want on a page and what their widths will be (they needn't be the same; you can have one wide one and two regular ones or three regular and one narrow one, for example), you want to "break up" their regularity by judiciously inserting your headlines, subheads, and art. Typography and graphic design is something that requires years of study and practice, and no part-time amateur will ever bring the inspiration and appeal to a page layout that a professional can, but if you are not in a position to enjoy that luxury you can always fall back on the major-minor principle.

- Try to have only one major headline and one or two minor headlines to a page.
- Use the "one-major, one-minor" photo principle.
- Use "dropped capitals" only for the first paragraph of a new story or article.
- Break up your copy with bold-faced subheads every 50 or 100 words if you can. Let the subhead clue the reader in on what's coming. (Subheads, if well written, should summarize the thrust of the copy when scanned quickly.)
- Insert only one bold-faced or color "shout" or "call-out" on a page. These are quotes lifted from the body of copy and enlarged for effect.
- "Wrap" your copy around your photos, charts, and shouts.
- "Silhouette" your photos now and then. Cut out those tired, drab backgrounds and bring people to the fore. This works well when you are stuck with a "firing squad" or "grip-and-grin" loser.

Finally, take the time to write clear, meaningful headlines that get your point across right away. Avoid any temptation to use a pun or other play on words. It's become a national disease. Take time, too, to write captions that convey a clear idea of what the picture is about and what the importance of the work being done is. There are no throwaway elements in communications.

Design is important. It must reflect the character of your organization and the content of the message. Get professional help. If you can't afford or find professional help, learn all you can on your own. In the meantime, you can depend on the guidelines above to keep you out of trouble. They may even win you an award.

## Check list

☐ Does your copy, publication, or audiovisual piece pass the "silent critic" test?

☐ What kind of message is your design, or lack of one, sending out?

☐ Are your copy, art, and design equal in quality?

☐ Have you let the designer, artist, or photographer tell you what they think will work best?

☐ Are the faces big enough in your photographs?

☐ Does the design and typography enhance your copy or overpower it?

☐ Will your piece's design stand out in a crowd?

☐ Is your page too "gray" or too busy?

☐ Is your body copy big enough for easy reading?

☐ Do your photos show people doing interesting things or are they the "firing squad" variety?

☐ Have you got enough "white space" around your copy, headlines, and art?

☐ Is there one dominant story and photo on each page?

☐ Are your headlines clear and free of puns?

☐ Do your subheads tell a story?

☐ Are your captions interesting and informative?

## *Exercises*

- Interview a graphic designer about his or her profession. Find out about costs and schedules.
- Visit a printing plant and ask for a tour and explanation of what they do.
- Get someone to show you how a desktop computer page-layout program works.
- Look around you. How many things can you see, big and small, that had to be designed by someone. How much work would you say was involved with the most complicated? The least complicated?
- Read at least one book each on the basic principles of graphic design and typography.
- Gather some samples of fund-raising publications from local nonprofit agencies, colleges, and hospitals. Which are the most attractive? Can you tell why?
- On a large pad of newsprint (at least 17" by 14"), analyze the layout of several brochures, newsletters, and magazines. Using a black magic marker, break down the elements on each page into their simplest shapes—rectangles, circles, etc. Reduce the printed matter to simple weighted lines, biggest and blackest for headlines, thinner and lighter for body copy. Divide the photos or other art into simple black and white shapes (make all grays black). Work quickly—a 4-page brochure shouldn't take more than a few minutes. Can you see the designer's logic?

# Chapter Fourteen

# The Impact of Computers on Fund-Raising Communications

COMPUTERS, both desktop and mainframe computers, have had a revolutionary effect on modern fund-raising. They play a key role in writing and publishing fund-raising material, in tracking and dispatching stewardship reports and letters, in prospect analysis and demographic studies of potential donors, and in campaign planning, execution, and follow-through. During the late eighties and early nineties, things happened so fast that most of us were still busy catching on to hardware and programs we were already using to notice what was taking place. Bigger memories, faster data transmission, easier image manipulation and generation, and virtually unlimited fonts and graphic design, moved desktop publishing from a relatively arcane concept to the state-of-the-art leader in visual and printed communications. By and large, many of us are using powerful, versatile word-processing and page-layout programs every day whose powers we may never fully explore or understand. In most offices, or even for those of us who work alone, there is a distinction among what we know we can accomplish with computers, what management expects us to accomplish, and what can really be done.

To keep things manageable, I'm just going to talk about the communications aspect of desktop publishing and its impact on the nature and character of fund-raising writing today.

## The good news is...

First of all, as with most technological advances, computers carry both a blessing and a curse with them. The blessing is that we can draft and complete proposals, case statements, letters, and steward-ship reports faster than ever before. The curse is that management thinks there is no limit to this productivity and, worst of all, that technological proficiency with computers is easily mastered. If we can outline, draft, revise, and print a proposal in three days, why not two in three days, or three in two days?

So what do we do when the letter that was wanted yesterday is now wanted the day before yesterday? Many modern managers cranked out of MBA programs still have the Mandarin-like philosophy that personal knowledge of, or hands-on experience with, the tools of the working class constitute a character deficiency of some sort. Because computers are here to stay and grow more versatile and complex each day in what they offer us, the fund-raising writer and his or her manager should have at least a bare-bones grasp of what programs will be most useful. When I leaped with joy into the world of computer owners with my first 512K Macintosh computer and ImageWriter printer, I thought "How much better can this get?" That was back in the days when I could still read and understand the computer magazines and newsletters that flourished immediately. Today, most popular computer magazines are comprehensible only to dedicated hacks. Even as costs go down and applications increase, the technological complexity needed for true proficiency is limiting the field in the use of some software. I simply don't have time to master all the ins and outs of my own primary word processing program. I guess I could, if I wanted to, spend two or three months experimenting and memorizing hundreds of key commands. (And although many commands remain the same from one manufacturer's program to another's and among programs by the same manufacturer, the mathematical limitations on keyboard combinations assures confusion at some point.) The best part of all this is, however, that you really don't have to be a computer expert to get the results you need as a fund-raising writer. A little expertise and some common sense go a long way.

But all users should have a clue as to when ambition becomes folly. The first sign of this is when trying to do something yourself on a computer becomes a problem instead of a solution. At this point you had better rethink the job, get more training, or call in the computer cavalry—the professionals who really understand what is going on and what can and can't be done with the equipment, people, and programs you're working with.

Assuming that you or the organization you are working for are both willing and financially capable of acquiring the equipment and programs needed for modern fund-raising communications, what skills do you need to know? The types of hardware and software available today cause the mind to boggle, but no matter what you buy, they will all share certain common aspects and this is what you should know about them.

# The basic hardware

### Computers
Desktop computers come in all sizes and price ranges. Some are small enough to fit into your hand or a briefcase; others take two people to set up and move. For writers, there are even hybrids called "word processors," a kind of cross between a typewriter and a computer, but available at about a third of a computer's price. Computers also change more often than the weather. The computer you buy today is already obsolescent. A new model will be on the way before your credit card charge clears the bank. Once you decide on a model and manufacturer, buy the newest, most powerful, and user-friendly product you can afford. By most powerful, I mean the model with the largest "hard drive" and random access memory. (Sorry, you'll have to learn about these things.) If the model you choose is designed to accommodate future memory expansion, so much the better. Also, buy the computer keyboard that offers the most alphanumerical combinations and special function keys. Equally important, get the monitor with the biggest color screen and highest number of pixels (points of light) you can afford. Make sure all three things—computer, monitor, and keyboard—are included in the quoted price. They aren't always.

### Auxiliary computer screens
If you are going to do a lot of desktop publishing using page layout and graphic design programs, you will probably need a monitor that can show one or two full-sized 8 1/2" x 11" pages. Scrolling around a small screen when you are working against a deadline or doing page layout every day is madness. In this case, you may or may not need a color screen, but if cost is not a consideration, get it.

## Printers

Printers come in a variety of forms ranging from dot matrix to ink jet or laser printers. I happen to still be using a dot-matrix ImageWriter II by Macintosh. This is okay for working on drafts, but I would never submit copy to a client that wasn't printed on a laser printer. Laser printers are essential if you need to produce camera-ready copy. Because more and more printers can work from disks with a copy of the project on it that you provide, even camera-ready copy is becoming a thing of the past. Buy the best quality laser printer with the highest number of dots per square inch you can (300 to 600 dpi is good).

## Scanners

Scanners come in sizes ranging from less expensive hand-held models to table-sized products than can handle full color and photo gray scales. The big ones can feed up to 100 pages through automatically. Scanners are most useful for entering large volumes of copy or graphic material directly into your computer. They are major time-saving devices, but something you can live without if need be.

## Modems and networking hardware

Modems link your computer with outside service networks and other computers as far away as you are willing to pay for. They can turn your computer and printer into a Fax machine. Files of any size can be sent back and forth from office to office or office to printer or printer to art agency in seconds. You can hook up to your local library or city hall records office if you have the access program for that sort of thing. Modems also let different types of computers "talk" to each other—Macs to IBMs in most cases. A modem program is needed as well as hardware but usually comes with the modem. Every office should have at least one modem. Buy the fastest one (in terms of bps or bytes per second) you can. The salesperson can advise you.

Networking hardware (usually a simple plug-in jack and a cable) links up all the computers in the office. It lets you share both information and software programs and leave messages in electronic mailboxes. If you have more than two computers in your shop, you'll want this option. (Some rewiring may be needed.)

# The most-used software applications

### Word processing

Remember carbon paper? Cutting and pasting? Correction fluid? Setting margins on the typewriter? No? Good. The programs available to writers today make outlining, writing, revising, and editing a pleasure. Not only do they take the misery out of writing's less gratifying chores, but they will even correct our spelling, give us a word count, check for redundancies, set up the pages, and make a table of contents and an index at the flick of finger or the click of a mouse. I still know people who write by hand with pen or pencil. I do it myself when I write a poem or a personal letter. There's a lot to be said for the tactile pleasure of putting words on paper that way, a greater feeling of craftsmanship perhaps. But when it comes to high-volume, time-sensitive writing, give me the computer every day in the week. I doubled my part-time income with my first Mac just because I could say "yes" more often. Another virtue of today's word-processing software is that they can usually convert something written in another maker's style by "saving" it as one of their own documents. The most expensive programs offer the most options, but lower-priced programs are so versatile that the average writer is just as happy with them. Ask your friends what they use and why.

### Graphic design

Here again, I'm from the old cut-and-paste school of making mechanicals for the printer. Drawing those blue pencil lines, pressing down transfer type and registration marks with a stylus, stripping in columns of typography from the printer with rubber cement, hand-drawing the boxes where the photos needed to be dropped in, then sending it all off to be converted into a repro stat. Hours, even days, of work, were necessary.

The page lay-out programs now available, even the simplest and least expensive, can do this and more in a matter of minutes. And they can do it in color. And they can plug in clip art or scanned photos in seconds. A page design can be set up, shifted about, and altered at will until the designer has the concept he or she was looking for. Typography and art are placed, moved, and generally handled with equal ease. Fund-raising operations can not only save money by doing some publications in-house, they can give a professional look to projects that were too low in volume to get printed originally.

### Scanning

Optical character reading packages have reached such a high quality level that almost any font is readable. Even mixed fonts can be scanned. It is no longer necessary to correct or re-enter large blocks of copy by hand. Another advantage is that any material you have in "hard" form in your files can be re-entered should your hard disk fail.

### Slide production

If you can type and point a "mouse," you can now make your own slide shows. Using programs with predesigned color formats and templates, professional quality slide packages can be put together on disk in a few hours and taken to a service agency for conversion to 35mm slides. Here again, it helps to know something about the basics of slide design and graphics (keep them simple). A good test—if you hold your slide up to the light at arm's length, you should be able to read it with ease. If you can't, the type and art are too small or there is too much material on the slide.

### Art and drawing

Unless you have special training in computer illustration, there is no way you will master the amazing software now available. It requires intensive study and constant use to become good enough and fast enough to make it worth the trouble. But, you can learn to use and place clip art or copy and alter photos for use in low-level brochures and newsletters. If you need something of better quality, hire a pro.

## The most common products

### Proposals and reports

These primary documents can now be packaged in clean, easy-to-scan, type-set forms that will make them stand out from the competition. Titles, headlines, subheads, and body copy can be set up as a "style" in advance. Most word-processing programs come with five or six standard classic fonts in normal, bold, and italic faces. This is more than enough. Charts, graphs, and even photographs can be inserted at will with the better programs. Even if you are working with the typewriter-page style (which many business persons seem to prefer) you can still do margins, double- and single-spacing, "bullets," dashes, and multiple columns faster, cleaner, and easier than was ever possible on your trusty old Royal or Remington. With some programs, you can even add that familiar click of key striking paper. (That's one thing I miss. Typewriters were more tactile than computers will ever be. But then, a pen is more tactile still.)

### Letters

Letters can now be planned in advance for different audiences, using the "mix and merge" to add names, addresses, and signatures to a variety of body copy. Gone is the chore of typing every single thank-you note or annual appeal letter by hand. If you are using a standard letterhead, the names of committee members, return addresses, and phone and fax numbers can be added in compatible fonts and faces wherever you'd like them on the page. Big typo found at the last minute? No problem. A new letter, ready for signing, can be dispatched in seconds. If you have a modem or networking link, you can even forward it someplace else for signing.

### Newsletters

Newsletters are valuable tools for reaching special audiences. If you need to stay in touch with donors, prospects, members, or a large number of staff and employees, an in-house newsletter is the way to go. Most page-layout programs come with several preformatted newsletter templates that can be adapted to your needs. Low-volume black-and-white editions can be set up on the computer, printed on the laser printer, reproduced on a copying machine, and distributed by mail in a matter of days.

### Brochures

Sometimes we need an informational brochure, but we don't need the 5,000 or 10,000 copies that justify calling in a designer and printer. Special papers are now available in one color and white that let a fairly proficient computer user take advantage of the prepackaged brochure templates in your page-layout program. An 8 1/2" x 11" page converts into a neat 6-page, double-folded brochure that slips right into a #10 envelope, jacket pocket, or briefcase. For slick, multicolor pieces with a hot contemporary format, call your designer.

### Donor recognition lists

These now become easy to assemble, maintain, and distribute. A list stored in the word-processing format can be dropped into the page-layout program and set into whatever font and column arrangement you like for inclusion with your regular newsletter, annual report, or other informational mailing. Donors can be divided into gift club categories or kept in simple alphabetical sequences with keyboard symbols added after the name to indicate special gift club levels.

# The advantages of using computers

### Speedy production
There is no question that the computer is a time-saving and labor-saving invention in the hands of a trained operator. But even your best worker can get swamped if requests and assignments are coming from every direction. Keep the work load reasonable and the chain of command intact.

### Lower costs
Most of the money you save on the publishing end will come by setting your own type in advance. If you do the design work yourself, too, your outfit will save even more. Managers sometimes forget to include hourly preparation and follow-through time in pricing an item produced internally. It's cheaper by computer, but it's not free. You will find that even though one person can do the work of what used to take two or three persons, since the old standards no longer apply, you can't figure that as a cost-saving. Unless, of course, you've been told to cut staff and keep production up anyway.

### Greater versatility
With computers, your communications operation can offer you a broad variety of options on how to produce and present material. How well this is done, is determined by the talents and skills of the communications staff and the receptiveness of management to innovation.

### Employee satisfaction
When people get the hang of using modern computers and the accompanying hardware and software that goes with them, they enjoy the freedom and gratification that comes with renewed creativity. After a while, brilliant solutions become second nature. But don't get too excited, people always find something to complain about.

### Rapid data transmission
With computers, modems, networking links, electronic mail, and Fax devices, we now send and receive more information in one day than was sent in the first 75 years of the century combined.

Whether this is good or bad remains to be seen. I don't know about you, but my brain kicks into the shut-down mode a lot faster that it used to do. It is already possible to submit proposals by computer to some corporations and foundations. I see this as becoming routine. God help the foundations and corporations on deadline day. Some years ago, I saw a slide of an National Institutes of Health warehouse on deadline day. It looked like an avalanche of 3-inch-thick proposals 12 to 15 feet high. No joke. At least with computers, we'll save on paper.

## Biggest obstacles to successful use of computers

### Lack of training
Most organizations can't afford to send their people out for private instruction, and workers themselves get so caught up in the flow of the workload that their knowledge of any one program is fragmentary. In a multicomputer office, there tends to be an uneven range of knowledge with one person eventually becoming a guru for the others. This means that the guru loses time from his or her own assignments. If you can get training, get it. Time lost from the office or the home workshop now will be more than recovered later. Managers, send your workers to all the computer workshops practical. They'll not only do the job better, but may come up with solutions and innovations that will make the office more productive. The knowledge they gain can be passed on to future workers.

### Learning curves
The learning curve for any given computer or program is much longer than most managers want to accept. Workers, too, will conceal a lack of knowledge hoping to make it up on the job. And who can blame them in today's market. Once a writer or publications worker achieves real skill in communications software, don't let them get away too easily. It may take months or even years to get back to old levels of productivity because of the learning curve inherent in today's software. As new software comes out, it tends to be more versatile but more complicated than before.

### Poorly written manuals
Even the best-written handbooks and operator's manuals usually miss something that turns out to be a key step in learning the system. I have always found, and probably you have too, that the

problem I am having in using a program is just the one they forgot to include. At other times, you'll get a manual that reads as if it were written and printed for an entirely different version of the program. Know why? It is. They haven't caught up with their own changes yet. And then there are the manuals you wonder why they took the trouble to write. I have friends who say they never read instructional manuals, but just wing it figuring out problems as they come up. I have always been skeptical about these claims. So should you.

### Program and hardware compatibility

Many offices share mixed types of hardware—IBM, Macintosh, and various kinds of clones. Frequently, too, different versions of the same programs are in use. One person may have the 2.0 version of a word-processing program while others are using 2.1 or 2.2. Even though newer hardware and newer programs can overcome these incompatibilities, try to keep everyone using the same type of machines and the same versions of software. It works out best in the long run, even if you have to spend a few dollars more to do this.

### Limited expertise

Some people seem to be incapable of rising above a certain level of skill with computers. Age and sex have nothing to do with it. It's just the way they work. Try to ascertain in advance just what skills people have. If, however, a really good writer isn't so hot on the machine, hire her anyway. That's the real talent. That's what you are paying for.

### Uneven skills among practitioners

I've pretty much covered this in the paragraphs above. What I want to say here is "Don't dump all the work on one or two persons just because they are more proficient with computers than the rest of the gang." Unless less-skilled workers are challenged and given the opportunity to catch up, they will become lazy and a source of contention in the office.

### Service and back-up availability

Computers, printers, and modems break down just like other machines. Ideally, you will have back-up units available. If you don't, you'd better have a service contract with a nearby maintenance and repair group. This is usually well worth the money, because the people who make their living this way have an intense interest in computers and can tell you many useful things about the programs you are using, including why they aren't doing what they are supposed to be doing.

### Physical discomfort

Don't spend more than 45 minutes or so at a computer console without getting up to stretch or take a walk. Muscular tension from staring at a monitor's screen can give a writer a blinding headache. Now that computers have been in use for some time, serious physical disabilities, such as carpal tunnel syndrome (an injury to the hands and wrists), are cropping up more and more. Use proper seating and posture and learn to do some of the tension-relieving exercises that can be done in place if necessary. If all that's too much to remember, just take a break as often as you can. Get up and walk away from the machine.

### Constant changes in the rules and the size of the playing field

By the time this book is printed, I expect major changes in the way computers are set up and operated. "Mice" will disappear. Voice-operated systems will be on the increase. Interactive "touch me" screens will be common and CD-ROM disks housing entire libraries will be available for a fraction of what they cost today. Eventually, the computer will become what it started out to be—a true extension of the human brain and nervous system. Don't panic. What you know now will still be valid for years to come. Just try to keep up and stay in touch with what's going on in our increasingly electronic society.

Jack Kerouac said that all a writer needs is a pencil and paper. True. But today desktop publishing sets the production standard everyone must compete against, and interactive electronic communications media are the wave of the future. The more you know today about computer hardware and software, and the more proficient you are in applying this knowledge to your fund-raising needs, the better chance you have for success in today's competitive fund-raising market. Get with the program.

## Check list

- ☐ Is your computer capable of doing all the things you need to do?
- ☐ Have you mastered the word processing, layout, and design programs you need to be productive and competitive?
- ☐ Do you need a full-sized color monitor for desktop publishing—one that can display two 8 1/2" x 11" pages?
- ☐ Can your printer produce "camera-ready" art and copy?

☐ Are you linked to other computers or services by modem?

☐ Is everyone you are working with using the same software version of your most-used programs?

☐ Are training programs available to improve your skills and those of colleagues?

☐ How about same-day servicing when the computer or the program crashes—can you get it?

☐ Do you take frequent breaks from keyboarding and do exercises to prevent discomfort or physical impairment?

## Exercises

- Visit the biggest computer sales center near you. Collect all the literature you can and have the salesperson demonstrate some of the word processing, reference, and page-layout programs for you. Get an idea of the minimum package—hardware and soft ware—that would meet your fund-raising writing needs.
- Visit the development office of the largest university or hospital near you. Find out how they use computers to fulfill their communications mission. Do they desktop their publications? What kind of hardware and software are they using? Are the computers networked? Do they work with outside designers and printers who work from their disks or get the information by modem?
- Take an introductory course in Macintosh- or IBM-type computers at the local evening school.
- Write to CASE, the *Chronicle of Philanthropy, Fund Raising Management*, or the national NSFRE offices for reprints of recent articles on the use of computers in fund raising.
- Read the "PC" magazines on library racks to get a feel for future directions in electronic communications.
- Check the "for sale" columns in the local newspapers for opportunities to buy a complete package of second-hand computer hardware and software. Recent college grads often don't want to lug the gear to another city, and you can get a real bargain. Or, perhaps, you might pick up last year's model cheap from some one who wants to trade up for one reason or another.

# PART THREE

# The Profession of Fund-Raising Writing

**Chapter Fifteen**

# An Approach to Fund-Raising Style–Part One

**S**tyle is how *you* write. Not how other people write. New writers spend more time worrying needlessly about what "style" they should use in writing something than they do in organizing and planning their approach to the job. As we gain in writing experience, patterns emerge in the way we choose words, shape sentences, and form them into paragraphs and pages. How this happens is determined by the writer's total life experience. What schools you attend, what teachers you have, what books you read. It's a life-long process, and, for the true writer a source of great pleasure. The true writer enjoys the blessing of strong powers of observation, an infallible ear for the nuances of speech and use of language, a reasonable degree of intelligence, an insatiable thirst for knowledge, great natural curiosity about many things, and a profound sense of honesty about his or her writing ability and the quality of work in progress. More than anything else, however, the true writer has an overwhelming compulsion to say something of lasting nature, to put words on paper that will interest, entertain, inform, inspire, and move others.

For money, if possible.

## On being a professional copywriter

Some people confuse the love of books with the love of writing and beautiful language. They are similar but not the same. There are many "successful" writers whose lack of familiarity with the works of great poets, novelists, playwrights, essayists, and historians is appalling. Ego and an implacable desire for success and public acclaim carry them forward. They are forgotten in a single generation. There are readers whose knowledge of literature and art is encyclopedic, but who never write at all.

The professional copywriter, a sort of amanuensis for the rest of humanity, writes the ad copy, the technical manuals, the government reports, and the thousands of speeches, letters, and proposals churned out every year so the wheels of business, education, and government can keep on turning, however slowly. The professional copywriter gathers the information and organizes the thoughts of high-placed administrators, officials, scientists, physicians, elected officials, bureaucrats, millionaire performers and ballplayers, and anyone else who needs to present information to the public in a cogent and appealing way, whether it be on paper or through the media. Copywriters do this by recognizing that *the essence of any successful communication is one person speaking to another*. Even the greatest orator, speaking over satellite TV to billions of people, reaches only one mind at a time.

Fund-raising writers are copywriters who deal in even more specific one-on-one assignments.

Their job is to be clear, interesting, precise and concise, and to make all the organization's written and spoken fund-raising communications speak with a single voice. They impose the fund-raising "style." Happily, almost anyone can learn enough about the language and techniques of fund-raising writing to do a respectable job.

- Good writing habits can be acquired and bad ones eliminated.
- Sensibilities as to what is acceptable and what is not will grow with experience.
- An understanding will emerge of the function and role of each type of fund-raising writing and how they relate to each other.

Without your realizing it, everything you need to know will come together. And it will be in your style. But…

There is no magic formula.

There are no secrets.

It's all common sense.

The key to good writing is liberation from your own fears and misconception about the use of language. The message Gertrude Stein had for us all was that we are free to do whatever we will with words, even if it's just to find out where they will take us and what we will discover on the trip.

# Why facts alone aren't enough

Just having the information isn't enough, said Jacques Barzun, in *Science: The Glorious Entertainment*, it's how you present that information. In development writing this means making your story engaging, accurate, and brief. It simply isn't good enough to say, "We're good. Send money." You've got to be able to show how and why your outfit's not only good, but the best one for the task at hand. And you've got to do it in a way the prospect will not only understand, but enjoy. If it doesn't please them, it won't interest them, Barzun said. Believe me, making your cause seem unique won't be easy. There are few really innovative ideas in the world today. Many things, especially in medicine and basic science, are essentially redundant. It's the *context* that counts.

But first you've got to get the information you'll need for writing that winning letter or proposal. Just as in house painting, preparation is indispensable to getting top-quality results. The first step should be setting up an interview with the key people involved with the project. The next is planning the interview itself to make sure no time is wasted and that you get useful answers to all the important questions. One way to guarantee this is to never ask a question that can be answered "yes" or "no." They will add nothing to your stock of information. Always ask something like, "Tell me why you decided to pursue this line of research," or "Who are the leading exponents of this theory?" Someone once said, "You can always tell the good scientists. They know right away when they're on the wrong track." The same can be said for a good fund-raising writer. He or she has the knack of keeping the conversation headed in the right direction. Digressions can be useful, true, but only as long as they amplify and enlighten the main idea.

# Conducting a productive interview

What about the structure of the interview? How many questions are enough? How many too many? What are the key questions to ask. Are there any good shortcuts to take?

First of all, you should always get at least an hour of the principal's time, and it doesn't hurt to give the interviewee at least a preliminary idea of what you'll be talking about and what supportive material you'll probably need. To do this, you'll have to take time to sit down and organize your own thoughts in advance. Make a list. Start with the major headings first and then fill in subquestions as you think of them. For example, if you are doing a proposal seeking research support, you'll want to know:

- What is the main goal of this project?
- Who are the principals involved?
- When do you plan to start, and how long will the project take?
- Where will the work take place?
- Why is this team the best one for this job?
- How much money do you need, and how do you plan to continue the work after the grant money runs out?

Ask questions, too, just to satisfy your own curiosity. These can lead to interesting details that make for good copy. Look for the person or persons behind the project. Sometimes you won't use any of this material, but the copy you do write will sound truer and more honest because of it.

- **It's okay to be dumb, too**. If you don't quite get the answer the first time, restate it or ask the person you're interviewing to put it in simpler terms. Don't *ever* try to guess at the meaning hoping you'll be able to figure it out later. You won't. And it will show. Don't pretend to know more than you do about the subject by throwing in an occasional word or two of jargon to impress your client. You may get buried under an avalanche of technical terms and allusions that will leave you hopelessly lost and embarrassed to boot.

- **If the interviewee talks too fast, tell him or her to slow down.** As many times as you need to. You may not get another chance at the interview. Ask the person you are interviewing to use a blackboard or a a piece of paper to illustrate points that are unclear. This will not only slow them down but give you some free reference material to use later on.

- **Take the best notes you can.** If you know shorthand or speed writing, you have a real advantage. If you don't, invent a system of your own. Transcribe your notes as soon as you can. Within the hour if possible. When you do that, a word or two jotted down in haste is enough to recall an entire line of thought. The next day, however, the entire concept may be unrecallable. Try to reorganize your notes as you transcribe them by putting key points down where they belong rather than in the random, unstructured sequence they invariably follow in the interview.

- **Learn to listen well.** Give the persons you are interviewing ample time to make their point and prod them only when they stray from the main issue. After a while, you'll be able to sense when what's being said is important or not. Don't depend on a tape recorder as your primary note-taking tool. Mechanical devices invariably fail you at the worst possible time, usually in the presence of the most important people. Mikes also seem to cause people to freeze up and be less open in discussing their work. What you're looking for is as much interviewee enthusiasm as you can inspire. Sometimes you can promote a bit of congeniality by asking the person you're talking to some personal questions about the things you see in their office or work space. Not only will the subject relax, but you will too.

- **As the interview progresses, ask for additional information**—like budget projections, names of other persons to speak with, relevant articles and books, photos and drawings, floor plans, resumes of chief people, and historical background on the organization—whatever you can think of that will make your job easier and enrich the content of your writing.

Ask everything you can. Get everything you can. In interviewing, stupidity is a virtue. The only dumb question is the one you fail to ask, and the only dumb request is the one you fail to make.

## Turning information into communication

Unless the tale is an exceptionally good one that deserves rereading, people usually read short stories and books for only one reason. They need to find out how the story turns out. Believe it or not, the same holds true for effective letters and proposals. It's the suspense that gets them every time. That's why a tiresome litany of pleas for "more support" and "needs that are greater than ever" will never succeed. Don't bore your reader to tears by the tired cliche of starting a writing project with the organization's history. Work it in later, if need be. You've got to draw the reader into the piece with just as much skill as a Stephen King or a Joyce Carol Oates.

This means you've got to do a bit of thinking yourself before you actually start to write. After all, just what does this project or program mean to you? If you can't get excited about it, why should anyone else? A bit of background research on your subject matter, especially if it's complicated, can shed valuable light down the dim halls of reason. As with everything in life, the more you know about something, the less scary and more interesting it becomes. And never regard your fund-raising writing assignments as a chore. Do that and you may as well start looking for another line of work.

Writing, no matter what kind, is always a creative act. It's the fund-raising writer's job to transform raw, unshaped facts into informative, entertaining, and persuasive copy. Challenge yourself and challenge your reader. And don't get uptight about style or your plan for developing your ideas. Chances are, whatever you think of first will be on the right track or close to it. If you start looking over your shoulder for the boss's opinion or try to please everyone, you're headed for big trouble. Trust your instincts. Learn to work with your material, no matter how slim or challenging it may be, and arrange it in a sequence that will build the greatest suspense.

Orchestrate!

Choreograph!

Direct!

## How to loosen up your thinking

Surprise the reader whenever and however you can. It doesn't have to be anything dramatic, just a well-placed piece of new information or a comment they didn't expect. Communication, after all, is the transmission of information not previously known.

In other words, without giving yourself an intellectual hernia, try to put a new twist on old approaches. I'm a painter in my spare time. One of the best things I learned while studying drawing was that you've got to work from the general to the specific, from the big shapes to the little ones. Accents and highlights come last when everything else is in place.

Rough in your thoughts first and don't lock in to anything from the get-go. Be as flexible and as loose as the sketcher trying to capture the "gesture" of a figure or object before he pins down the details. One way to do this is to use "visual thinking" and free association to loosen up your approach. Before you start to write, get a pad of newsprint at your art supply store and a couple of soft black pencils. Start doodling the words, shapes, and objects that pop into your mind as your review your notes. Link the ones that seem to relate to each other with lines and boxes. Don't make judgements about what they may or may not mean. Just do it. When you run out of ideas, look for the dominant themes. You'll feel the scales falling away from your preconceived thoughts and ideas. Keep adding new doodles as they occur. Study them too. Where do they fit in?

Sometimes the best way to see something is to look at it from a different angle.

## Don't be afraid to radically reorganize your draft

There's an old saying that if you want to have your story or article accepted by the *New Yorker*, the best thing to do is to: 1) throw away the first and last pages; 2) throw the rest of the manuscript down a set of stairs; and 3) Retrieve them in the order they landed, starting from the top or bottom as the mood strikes you.

That's one way to reorganize. I usually do something like the following:

> If, as you reread copy, something strikes you as being out of place, draw a box around it and write "move?" next to the box. When you discover where it belongs, mark the place it goes with a number or letter, then tag the box with the same letter, i.e., "move to A" or "move to #1." If you can't figure out where a piece of copy belongs, it probably doesn't. Scrap it.

The *New Yorker* advice aside, the best openings or "leads" often do turn up in the second or third paragraph, or even later. If you like a piece of copy better up front, move it. You're in charge, aren't you? At least till you turn in the copy. Whenever you're clearly uncomfortable with a passage, change it, move it, or kill it. If you're not sure, leave it in the first draft. The editor or reviewer will either confirm your opinion or let it stand. But don't make a habit of depending on this method to solve all your problems. It won't work. You'll just become a sloppy writer. Some writers do their best writing in the rewriting process. Others, like Gerald Durrell, hardly change a line. For most of us, however, revision and editing come with the territory. Don't shy away from reorganizing illogically sequenced copy.

## Know when to stop

How long is long enough in any piece of writing? How long is too long? I can't tell you how many times I am asked these two questions at seminars and roundtables. The answer I usually give is that a proposal or letter or any other piece of fund-raising copy should have just enough information and just enough inspiration to make the reader decide in your favor. This means writing clear, tight copy with as little embroidery as possible. Taking things out almost always helps the copy more than putting things in. If you follow the guidelines below, you will see exactly what I mean and almost automatically come up with the right length for each project. And I'll tell you a secret. You can tell when you're doing things right, because all of a sudden you're having fun.

## Check List

☐ Do you list and organize your interview questions in advance?
☐ Do you control the pace of the interview?
☐ Do you take good notes and transcribe them immediately?

- ☐ Do you listen well?
- ☐ Do you ask for supporting material or references?
- ☐ Have you researched the subject enough before beginning to write?
- ☐ Have you worked from the general to the specific in structuring your draft?
- ☐ Have you revised and reorganized your draft to make the copy flow better?

# Chapter Sixteen

# An Approach to Fund-Raising Style–Part Two

**T**HE great thing about the English language is no matter how badly you screw it up, people still usually know what you mean. So far, only lawyers, academics, physicians, the federal government, and the people who write insurance policies have been able to overcome this advantage. Unfortunately, the rest of the English-speaking world seems determined to join them. The greatest problem for the fund-raising writer is that so many people he or she has to work with are used to gobbledygook, they don't know clear, effective writing when they see it. Sometimes, clients seem incapable of grasping the few simple rules that improve copy readability.

If it is true that the average reader is in trouble about half the time, writers have to help them out. Otherwise, the message will be lost.

"Good writing," said George Orwell, "is like a pane of glass." What he meant was that the writing shouldn't get in the way of the thought expressed. Here are seven important, easy-to-remember "rules" to keep people reading your copy:

- **Make an outline** for anything you write
- **Use short words** more than long words
- **Use words with Anglo-Saxon roots** more than words with Latin or Greek roots
- **Use active verbs.**—they are more exciting and interesting than passive ones

- **Use adjectives, adverbs, and intensifiers sparingly**
- **Be selective**—what you leave out is as important as what you put in
- **Know your basic grammar**—it's okay to be ungrammatical if you do it knowingly and for a purpose

Good writers seem to do these things almost instinctively. But the secret is that professional writers go over and over their copy for hours looking for ways to improve it and make it easier to read and retain. You should too. If you are lucky enough to have a good word-processing program for your computer, it will make checking and changing things much faster.

With these thoughts in mind, let's talk about some of the "rules" above.

## Make an outline for anything you write

This rule seems so basic that it's hard to believe how many people don't follow it. People usually pick up their pen, roll a sheet of paper into a typewriter, or sit down at a computer and start at the top. They hope, or assume, I suppose that everything will flow once they are possessed by the muse. It doesn't work like that. First of all, you've got to be rock-solid sure that your copy will have an intriguing beginning, a fascinating middle, and a satisfying end. You want to make sure that you cover all the key points in whatever it is that you are writing. This means you've got to list them in the order that you want the reader to hear about them. To do this takes planning.

When you outline, list all the key topics or elements in the forms of little headlines that will help you write the paragraph that follows. If you do it right, taken together, those "headlines" will tell a story in themselves. You may even want to use them in the final copy. If you don't know where to start, just write down all the thoughts that come into your head as you think of the problem at hand. Don't judge them, just write them down. Do it until you can't think of anything else. Put them away overnight. Absolutely don't look at them for 24 hours. Later, when you go over them, rearrange them into the sequence that seems natural. Some will become major section headings. Others will fall beneath these as subheadings. You will be amazed at all the new material that will suddenly occur to you as you go along. In no time at all, you will discover that the piece you are working on is suddenly shaping itself. Any material that is missing or skimpy will be all the more apparent to you as well.

## Use short words more than long words

This applies to words, sentences, paragraphs, and documents. I am not saying that you must *always* mechanically shorten your writing. I am telling you to make it as lean and tight as you can when you can. That way, when you must take more time and space to discuss or explain a point, you will do it by design, rather than by accident. There is no excuse for rabbiting on pointlessly in fund-raising copy. Never use three, four, or five words when one word will do, e.g., "a large number of" instead of "many." When you do write long sentences or paragraphs, use the short sentence or paragraph for contrast or to underscore your meaning.

It works.

See.

To know if your copy is lean and readable enough without counting the words in every sentence on every page, try the following: Take a full page of typescript and count all the words on the page. Then go back and count all the words that are five letters or less. (Verbs ending in "ed" or "ing" qualify if their stem is five letters or less.) Divide the total number of words on the page into the total number of words that are five letters or less to get the percentage of five-letter words. If this comes out to 70 percent or more, your copy is probably readable. For example, if 180 words out of 250 have five letters or less, that's 72 percent. You're okay. In spite of what academics and others would have you believe, most persons prefer to read at a couple of levels lower than their educational level. It's less work. (In case you were wondering, most of the words in this book are four to five letters long.)

## Use Anglo-Saxon words more than words with Latin or Greek roots

The reason that Anglo-Saxon words work well is because they are short.

"Book" is shorter than "publication."

"Get" is shorter than "acquire."

"Walk" is shorter than "perambulation."

"Show" is shorter than "demonstrate."

"About" works just as well as "approximately."

Proof that we Americans prefer short words to long ones can be seen in our tendency to chop words down to manageable sizes. TV is easier to say and write than television. We call our physicians "Doc" and our policemen cops. And we go to school, not to university. Well, you get the drift. Just for the drill, take a page from a college-level textbook and replace all the long Latin- and Greek-root words with their shorter Anglo-Saxon cousins. See how much easier the material is to read? (Generally speaking, the more degrees a person has, the more high falutin' he or she will write. It's an occupational hazard.) According to Bill Bryson, author of *The Mother Tongue*, although only about 4,500 Anglo-Saxon words have survived in modern English usage, they just happen to be some of the most important (and shortest) words in the language: love, eat, drink, house, at, to, for, in, and so on. Bryson, citing other sources, notes that *every one of the 100 most-used words in English are Anglo-Saxon in origin*. And we use less then half of these in daily communication. If you're wondering how this can be true, just think how few letters there are in an alphabet or how few notes there are in musical transcription. It's all in how they're put together and expressed.

## Use active verbs—they excite and interest readers more than passive ones

Passive verbs, by their nature make sentences longer and limper. "The man bit the dog" is shorter by two words than "The dog was bitten by the man." It gets to the point faster and more forcibly. There is nothing wrong with passive constructions. In fact, many times they are more graceful and effective than a direct statement. What is wrong, however, is to use them to excess. Physicians, scientists, and PhDs in general do this more than other writers, usually to avoid indicating who is doing or saying something. Almost without fail, they will write "It is believed that, etc.," or "It has been observed, etc.," rather than say "I believe," or "I observed." (For some reason, they think this makes their work more objective.) A writing habit closely related to excessive use of the passive voice is to turn perfectly good verbs into substantives. Rather than say "the factory produces widgets," the wordy writer says "the factory is engaged in the production of widgets." Keep an eye out for the "of" word. Chances are it's preceded by four or five words that can be replaced with a single active verb.

Watch out, too, for too many uses of the verb "to be" and other linking verbs. You'll profit from replacing the "is," "are," "was," and "will be" with some other verb form. For example, if you have written "The president will be advised that you are willing to participate," try "We'll tell the president you want to help."

## Use adjectives, adverbs, and intensifiers sparingly

Modifiers should only be used if they make the writing clearer and more precise. They should never be used for the sake of filling up space or trying to make weak sentences stronger and routine ideas or facts sound like more than they are. Outlining your copy before you start to write will cut down on this tendency. For most of us, however, it's a matter of going back over the copy and revising till it hurts.

Incidentally, when you change your own copy, it's called revising, when you take an axe to somebody else's masterwork, it's editing. Either way, if removing any word or phrase fails to change the meaning of the sentence, it probably didn't belong there in the first place. In nearly every case, you'll get a clear feeling that the sentence is stronger and easier to read than it was in its original form.

## Be selective—what you leave out is as important as what you put in

Never tell anybody everything you know. Leave a little mystery to your copy. Always leave the reader wanting more. The human brain has an amazing capacity for filling in perceived gaps with "information" far more forceful than any minor detail you might throw in in an effort to be thorough. Tell him or her too much at the wrong time and place and you'll not only lose your reader, you'll lose the emotional tie they may be forming with the ideas being presented. We all have one or two friends who are "boring on a broad range of subjects." When you are working on something, ask yourself, "Would I really want to know all this?"

## Know your basic grammar—it's okay to be ungrammatical if you do it knowingly and for a purpose

One of my favorite jokes is based on how we all feel about people who correct our grammar, usually in a niggling way. There was a knock at the Pearly Gates. "Who is it," says St. Peter. "It is I," says a voice from without. "Well, I'm afraid you'll have to go to hell," says St. Peter, "We have too many English teachers in here already."

If you want to begin a sentence with "and" or "but" do it. Use a fragmentary sentence if it gets the point across. Any point. Use contractions. Split an infinitive. End a sentence with a preposition. Shakespeare did. So did Churchill. These last two points are myths, anyway. Told that he couldn't end a sentence with an preposition, Churchill allegedly said, "This is something up with which I shall not put!" Which not only takes the steam out of the criticism but shows what happens to a sentence when you bend over backwards for form's sake. The language is ours to use as we please. But only if we know the rules we break. It's every writer's business to know the tools of the trade. Grammar may, indeed, be a "body of rules surrounded by exceptions," but grammar, spelling, and syntax are fundamental and worth the time it takes to study and master.

In addition to these seven fundamental practices, there are other things you should do to sharpen your material.

- Look for redundancies, misspellings (especially names), and punctuation errors. Check your copy. Watch out for pet words and phrases that creep in over and over again. Even if you are sure of the spelling or usage that looks a bit odd, check it. It's probably wrong.
- Strive for clarity of thought and felicity of expression. Can you understand what you just said? Be sure that you got it right. Does your copy sound as good as "Tiger, tiger burning bright in the forests of the night" (William Blake) or "The woods are lovely, dark and deep?" (Robert Frost). Now that's felicity.
- Ask a disinterested person to read your copy for general sense. He or she will spot things you've missed five or six times.
- Listen to his or her comments and consider them carefully. If a person says they don't understand something or suspect your command of the language is less than it might be, don't get sore. Fix the copy.
- Revise and rewrite with the seven fundamental rules in mind. No one will ever complain if there is less to read and more time to read it in.

## Some personal advice

Stupid words and practices abound in writing. They always have and they always will. How can you spot these useless words and phrases? I can't possibly list all of them, and, in fact, it's better that you learn to spot them for yourself. (To paraphrase Ernest Hemingway, every writer needs a built-in crap detector.) I can tell you that, without exception, they tend to be ugly, awkward, and inexact. This alone should warn you to get rid of them. For instance:

- Don't use the word "ongoing" when you mean "continuing," or phrases like "impact upon" when you mean "affect,"
- Don't say "comprise" when you mean "compose." (The one big thing always comprises the many little things, e.g., "The navy comprises aircraft carriers, cruisers, destroyers, and sub-

marines." Not the other way around.) There is no such construction as "comprised of."

- Don't say "infer" when you mean "imply." (I imply something and you infer from what I said.)
- Don't write "alot." It's two words, "a lot."
- You don't "belabor" a point. You labor it. Belabor means to beat about the head.
- Don't say "like" when you mean "such as."
- Never use the word "hopefully." You'll be wrong.
- Compare similar things to one another (chestnuts to walnuts); compare dissimilar things *with* one another (apples with oranges). Shakespeare gets it wrong too, for example, "Shall I compare thee to a summer's day?"
- Never use the legalistic atrocity "and/or" which implies three possible choices. ("John and/or Mary will do it." can be interpreted to mean that: 1) John will do it; 2) Mary will do it.; or 3) They will both do it. Take time to write out exactly what it is you mean. ("John will do it, and if he can't Mary will." You will find that "and" or "or" will do by themselves. Never foist a dilemma upon your reader. They are easily enough confused and troubled as it is.
- The singular possessive of a singular word ending in "s" calls for an apostrophe plus another "s." Thus, a painting by Thomas Eakins is Mr. Eakins's painting. The daughter of the boss is the boss's daughter. Even though many magazines and newspapers, some of them reputable, fail to do this, it is the sign of a brain-dead writer with no ear for the language and no sense of nuance.
- Use the serial comma or not as you wish, but be consistent. (That means you can put a comma before the word "and" in a series of three or more. For example, "red, white, and blue.") "And" unifies elements in a sentence, a comma separates them.
- Avoid excessive capitalization, especially of titles. It makes sentences harder to read and Germanic in appearance.
- Learn the correct use of hyphens. It's a tricky business, but in general, if compound words come before a noun they need a hyphen. If they follow it, they don't. For instance, "I can tell you some *fund-raising* tricks, but not all I know about fund raising." or "The *eight-year-old* boy was just like any other *eight year old*." Get it? Well-informed writers will.
- Watch out for modifying words and phrases that hit the wrong target. ("I shot an elephant in my pajamas...")
- Make sure your verbs agree with your nouns: plural with plural

and singular with singular.

- Pick a style manual and stick to it. The *New York Times Style Book* and the *Chicago Manual of Style* are the best of the bunch. (Never use a style book that tries to tell you the singular possessive of a word ending in "s" only needs an apostrophe.)
- Read books on the craft of writing including poetry and drama to enrich your knowledge and heighten your sensitivity.
- Read some good books about the origins and use of English. Above all get the little book called *The Elements of Style* by Strunk and White. It has all the advice you'll ever really need about writing. Read Harold "Sy" Seymour's *Designs for Fund Raising*. His advice on language, length, and content for things like proposals and case statements is unsurpassed. Lester King's *Why Not Say It Clearly* has great tips for simplifying medical and scientific material. Take a look at books on philology like Bill Bryson's *The Mother Tongue* or *The Story of English* by McCrum, Cran, and MacNeil. They'll not only show you how we got in the mess we're in with English, but show you how to find your way out of it. Read anything by Jacques Barzun, but especially *The Modern Researcher* and *Science, the Glorious Entertainment* if you can find them.

These authors will probably lead you to other writers and sources that will help to shape and sharpen your skills. And you'll need all the help you can get after the critics and language Nazis start closing in on your drafts and revisions.

There are thousands of other minor writing tips and suggestions I could give you, but it is better that you seek out or discover them on your own. English is the language of subtlety and nuance. You'll have to learn its ins and outs on your own and use them in ways appropriate to you. But you'll never learn them all, I promise you. The key thing is to know where to find help when you need it, and I think I have at least given you a start on that.

# Check list

☐ Have you outlined your copy and made subheads for the key points?

☐ Does your copy pass the 70% test for words of five letters or less?

☐ Do you prune out words with Greek and Latin roots when they are not needed and use shorter Anglo-Saxon words in their place?

☐ Are there too many passive and linking verbs in your copy?

☐ Have you reduced or eliminated unneeded adjectives, adverbs, and weak intensifiers?

☐ Have you been selective in choosing the information you wish to convey?

☐ Are you using certain words too often?

☐ Did you double-check your spelling and punctuation?

☐ Did you ask a third party to read your copy for general sense and readability?

☐ Do you really know the correct meaning of all the words you've used or are you shaky about a few? Look them up.

☐ Do you really know when and where to use the hyphen?

☐ Do your verbs and nouns agree?

## Exercises

- Rewrite several paragraphs from an academic, professional, or scientific journal article with four- and five-letter Anglo-Saxon words. Change all passive verbs to active verbs. Remove all adverbs and adjectives. How does the material look and sound now? Has any meaning been lost?

- For one week, when reading anything write down all words whose meaning you don't know or are unsure of. Look them up. Mentally use them correctly in two or three sentences.

- Take a course in speed writing or shorthand at the local evening school.

- Interview several professional people—lawyers, physicians, engineers, or scientists—about their careers and how they feel about what they do. How much good material did you come up with? What's missing? What's the human interest angle in what they told you?

- Do some "visual thinking" on paper about the big current news story in the papers. What did you come up with that outlining alone wouldn't reveal?

- Read a book on the source of English words and their original meanings.

- Memorize one of Shakespeare's sonnets. Find the rhythm in the language. Note how rich the intellectual and visual content is. Can you do as much in sixteen lines?

# Chapter Seventeen

# Advice to Clients, Freelancers, and Beginners

I N this book a "client" is anyone to whom the writer provides a service, whether as an independent freelancer or as a staff writer assigned to a particular project. This chapter deals with the relationship between freelance writers and their clients, but the information is useful for staff writers too.

## Advice to the client

While more and more writers are turning their hands to fund-raising writing, thanks to intensive competition for funding support today, most good ones have probably been spoken for. You can find them working for large universities and consulting firms. Experienced freelancers often command a hefty fee. What you get in return for this fee, however, is usually well worth the price. First and foremost, you will save a great deal of time lost through unproductive meetings and initial drafts that are far off the mark. You will probably finish the job sooner because an experienced writer knows from scratch what goes into, and what is best left out of, a good piece of fund-raising copy. Also, since the copy will be sharper, tighter, and more effective, yields will probably be higher and the cost relatively lower. For example, if you contract to pay an experienced writer to do a case statement and the piece helps to generate millions of dollars, you will clearly be well ahead of the game. The more the experience you buy the stronger the copy and the fewer the mistakes.

A good fund-raising writer will give you a piece with more sparkle and freshness. He or she will winnow out the chaff and highlight the most important points in the most effective way. After they read the case, you will probably hear colleagues saying things like, "Gee, are we really this good?"

How long should it take for a writer to finish a draft? Obviously, it depends on the job's length and complexity. A case statement will take months by the time everyone has a say. Maybe even a year. A letter, by contrast, can be turned around in a day or two. Most proposals, for some reason unknown to me, seem to average about six weeks from the discussion stage to the final draft.

By rule of thumb, the more people that have to okay a project, the longer it will take. When in doubt, take the amount of time you thought it should take to finish a job, and raise it to the next highest time unit. For example, if you're planning a direct mail package that you would like to see go out the door in a couple of weeks, raise that to a couple of months, and you'll have the worst case scenario.

- Before you call in a writer **be sure you have a clear idea what your goal is** and what it means to your organization's success. If you don't know what your message is, no writer can help you.
- Tell the writer what **the project is** about and how it fits into the big picture.
- Work out a **specific budget** and **timetable** for your writing project.
- Make sure the writer and other participants get this and other related material **before the first meeting**.
- Have the writer **meet the principal parties**.
- **Set a deadline** for the first draft.
- **Be handy for follow-up questions**.
- Reserve **right of review and comment to as few persons as possible**. A senior executive and the project manager should do.
- Give the writer **time to assess the job** and submit his or her cost estimate and timetable. **Be sure it's in writing**.
- Keep in mind that writers try to make your material as easy to understand as possible. Before changing anything arbitrarily, **be sure your way will truly improve the copy**. (The greatest human urge is not for power, money, or sex. It is the uncontrollable desire to rewrite something someone else has just written.)
- Be **honest when reviewing the copy**. Tell the writer exactly what you do and don't like.

- When the work is done, **pay the bill promptly**. It shows that you appreciated the effort and will make the writer happy to work with you again.

## Advice to freelance writers

Writers, in submitting their bids, should itemize what the client will get, when the client will get it, and what, if any, fees he or she will be charged for killing a project in midstream. For example, if a publication is involved, a bid might include the copy, headlines, photo captions, call-outs (highlighted selections of text), proofreading, and one full revision. (I usually invoke a 70 percent "kill fee." This protects me from any losses caused by work I was unable to take on during the period set aside for the job. It also guards against frivolous employers who seem to think a writing contract is different from hiring a house painter or buying a piece of real estate.) Writers should specify how long they think the job will take in terms of days or hours. Usually, "40 to 50 hours" or "five to six days" will do the trick.

There are some other things you need to do, some of which are obvious, some not:

- **Meet your deadline**. This is always professional rule number one.
- **Never make any commitment about a proposal's, or any other project's, chances for success**. If the client has a sound project and prospect research is on the mark, a well-prepared, well-documented, well-written piece submitted well in advance of the deadline has as much chance as anyone else's. No more, no less.
- **Always press for as many interviews and as much written background data and information on your project as you can get**. Never, never let someone pawn off a half-baked, undocumented, and unbudgeted project on you hoping that you will solve their problem. Too many "proposals" result from someone being pressed to "do something" and do it soon.
- **Always insist on as much time as you need** to complete your interviews, do research, and write your first draft. Don't be rushed into fast turnarounds.
- **Nail down budget details at the start.**
- **Deal directly with people as high on the totem pole as you can**, but talk to support staff too. Sometimes they are the only people who really know what is going on.
- Be aware that your client has good **reasons** for wanting things to be **said in a particular way**.

- If you are working on a writing job and find yourself coming into conflict with some of the principles over the way your material is presented, a point of grammar or usage, or are just having a personality conflict a good rule for all fund-raising writers to remember is "**Never be right more than 80 percent of the time**." Translation: Choose your battles cautiously. Never go to war over an issue unless there is no other way out. Not if you want to work there again.

The worst thing you can do is get discouraged when you don't get an assignment, or when an assignment you turn in is trashed by the development editor or one of his or her bosses. I have seen truly excellent, fresh, innovative copy by writers of both stature and experience brutally criticized by inexperienced and ill-informed academic deans. These writers did what all true professionals do. They went on to the next assignment. If you think you can't take this kind of punishment, maybe you should think about another line of work.

Once you get an assignment, don't slavishly imitate the style of fund-raising materials you may have seen elsewhere, borrowed, or come across in the library's collection of foundation and fund-raising information. It's one thing to be familiar with this stuff; it's another to parrot it. Every editor likes to see someone who can put a new spin on old material. Originality counts big. The big drawback in writing development copy is that you don't use all your "mental muscles." To keep your outlook—and your writing skills—from getting dull, write for as many other purposes as you can. Write poetry, one-act plays, essays, speeches, short stories, novels, mysteries, ad copy. Anything that will sharpen and renew your language skills.

## Advice on payments and fees

How much to charge? How much to pay? The answers to these two questions will vary depending on the part of the country you're in and the going rates there. Time, too, will influence costs. Writers have a right to raise their fees for rush jobs which interrupt their regularly scheduled assignments and put extra pressure on them and their relationship with supporting resources such as photographers, designers, and printers. As a rule, writers base their fees on what they estimate to be a reasonable amount of time to finish the job, plus a buffer of time to account for unexpected or additional changes, additions, or revisions. Normally, no writer should be expected to do more than one revision of the first draft for the original fee. Failure to establish that up front will lead to endless delays caused by constant noodling with each revision. Experienced writers will have a clear idea of what their time is worth, including overhead costs and expenses if they are a full-time free lancer. This will enable them to submit a fixed-price bid for the job. In general, a fixed price works best for both writer and client. The writer can pencil in his projected earnings more easily and the client knows exactly what the job will cost him well in advance of the bill coming due. The added advantage to the writer is that an early finish will increase his profit margin without detracting from the quality of the work, while the client has a guarantee that no matter how long the first draft, plus revisions, actually takes, he or she won't get socked with unexpected costs.

Conversely, clients should have some idea of how much they are willing to spend for a particular piece of writing. This will enable them to: 1) make a firm offer to the writer and let him or her make the decision to take or turn down the assignment or; 2) establish the basis for negotiating a lower cost if the writer's ask is over budget.

To me, any contract based on an open-ended hourly rate is unfair to both sides: a slow, inefficient writer will wind up making more money for a given job than a fast, effective one. The client, on the other hand, will not know until the last minute how much of the writing budget will be consumed by the hourly rate assignment. Based on my experience, I believe the fixed price bid is best. Where pricing is concerned, the right price for writers is the one that makes them happy to do the job; for clients, it is the one they feel most comfortable paying.

## Advice on avoiding problems

Sometimes a client has unrealistic expectations about what can be accomplished through a piece of fund-raising copy. Some of these expectations are the writer's fault, some of them just come with the territory.

For instance, the client may often be naive about how long it takes to produce something and what such products and services actually cost. After discussing the project, let's say a proposal to a corporation to help increase volunteering in communities served by their business, the writer and the client should be in agreement about goals, deadlines, and potential results. Both should have a clear picture of what's expected.

But sometimes writers promise results over which they have no control, such as the likelihood of receiving a gift or grant, how much may be received, and how soon it can be expected. Anxious to please and be agreeable, or simply in need of cash, writers often accept scanty or inadequate information on which to base their work and agree to unreasonable deadlines for drafts and final copy. Failure to deliver a satisfactory product for any of these reasons erodes the writer's credibility and strains future relationships with the client.

A related problem, but a common one, is low client regard for the writer's ability to grasp the details and significance of the proposed work. Skepticism increases when projects involve scientific or technical material. After all, how can someone with a liberal arts bachelor's degree possibly navigate the ins and outs of molecular biology or quantum physics? In fact, they don't have to. They only have to find out, with the help of the experts, what the outcome of this work means to society and present it in cogent, readable terms. Mutual trust and respect are indispensable to producing good material.

These suggestions may seem simplistic, but they prevent misunderstandings, avoid delays, and smooth the writing process.

## Tips for newcomers–how to break in and find work

The first thing any employer looks for in a writer is experience. In fund raising, notably, nothing replaces experience.

Except talent.

If you, as a prospective employer, can find neither the budget nor the writer you want, don't be afraid to take a chance on a talented youngster. A talented writer can learn fund-raising writing inside and out in about two years.

If, as a young or new writer, you feel you lack experience in the development field, don't knock yourself out of the box. Take whatever writings you have accumulated, especially anything in print (even if it's the college newspaper or literary magazine), and get yourself interviewed.

### How I got into the game

Most experienced fund-raising writers, including me, will tell you that they more or less drifted into the field as they built on earlier experiences. In my case, I started out as an assistant editor at *Business Week* where I soon learned to favor medical- or science-oriented stories over straight business articles. (Mainly because I didn't know or care much about business; I didn't know much about science either, but there was at least a human interest side to it.)

After a couple of years, the University of Pennsylvania offered me a job as chief science public relations officer in their News Office. From there, I moved over to the University's

Development Office as a senior writer. Along the way, I had been writing freelance science copy for ad agencies, marketing outfits, and research organizations. As a development writer, I continued to specialize in medical and science projects, but tackled the liberal arts and business school projects, too. I was fortunate enough to be there for Penn's $255 million *Program for the Eighties* which let me take on every kind of task from case statements and proposals to stewardship reports, brochures, and annual fund letters. About seven years later I moved to Thomas Jefferson University to become chief of development communications for their $65 million *Decade Fund Campaign*. I later laid the communications groundwork for a $200-million *Jefferson 2000 Fund* drive, before starting my own consultancy in fundraising communications. All told, including consulting jobs, I have had a hand in raising more than $500 million dollars over the last couple of decades. (It has gone by fast. Development writing, with all its projects, schedules, and deadlines can make life seem even shorter than it is.)

The point is, even long-term professionals still work on professional skills through reading, attending or conducting seminars and conferences, and consulting.

### Make contact

The only way to find out if you have what it takes to be a fundraising writer is to keep going back into the marketplace. Getting a job or a freelance assignment is as much a matter of timing as it is of luck. The more you keep in touch, whether it's by phone or letter, the more you will come to mind to potential employers. One of the best ways to become a face instead of just a name or a voice, is to ask for an "informational interview." Try to get an appointment (or better yet, a free lunch) with the director of development or the director of development communications. Tell them you would like to learn about some of the requirements of a writing position and what kind of job potential exists in the development field. Plead innocence. Even if you don't get a job lead, you'll know a lot more than you did before. You'll have new leads to other persons (ask for tips on where to go and who to speak with elsewhere) and new names to drop. If you can't talk to the boss, talk to the boss's assistant or the receptionist. As an old intelligence operator for the National Security Agency, I know how small bits of information add up. Stay in touch with the people you get to know. Persistence, and belief in yourself and your ability, are the greatest virtues you can have. If you don't believe you can do it, who will?

As professional fund raising for nonprofit organizations continues to become more important to the American economy, opportunities for jobs in fund-raising writing will increase.

If you can afford it, join organizations where you will get to meet and hobnob with established fund raisers. The National Society of Fund Raising Executives, the Council for the Advancement and Support of Education, the Public Relations Society of America, the American Medical Writers Association, and the American Association for the Advancement of Science are groups you might look into, given whatever particular field of fund-raising you hope to work in. If you can't afford a membership, try to attend the many short-course seminars given at local universities and colleges. You can find out where these are offered by calling or writing the local branch of the National Society of Fund Raising Executives. (They will know what openings are available and may have a placement newsletter they can send you.)

### Some of the jobs

If you are fresh out of college or have maybe a year's related experience, you can think about trying to become a research assistant or an assistant stewardship writer. The research writer investigates prospects, including corporations and foundations as well as individuals, and provides development officers with written evaluations and reports on such things as the subject's giving patterns and practices over time. The stewardship writer composes acknowledgment letters for the signature of organizational officers that allow quick response to gifts of all sizes. Often, this person drafts reports to major donors on the results and consequences of their gift. Both of these jobs are vital to sustaining a healthy fund-raising operation, and because these kind of writers soon become well grounded in the identities and background of donors pivotal to the nonprofit's success, they often become candidates for promotion to greater responsibilities. In fact, the nature of these jobs alone will encourage you to seek higher levels.

Eventually you can work your way up to a senior development writer's job with increasing responsibilities for direct-mail appeals, proposal letters, and publications work. As time goes by, you can look for a promotion to director of development communications, a job which has direct input into fund-raising policy making, planning, and decisions. At this level you will be writing major case statements and campaign plans. If writing is all you are interested in, this is probably where you will stay, unless, perhaps, you go on to become director of a university's entire communications group embracing marketing, public relations, and fund raising. Such things happen.

For those to whom writing isn't reward enough, with study and guidance, you can branch out to become a major gifts officer, a corporate or foundation relations person, director of the alumni program, a planned gifts expert, and eventually director or vice president for development for the entire organization.

### Some of the benefits

Development writing and development jobs in general pay better salaries than most comparable institutional and nonprofit positions. And well they should. Because it's a field where your performance can be measured in exact dollars and cents at the end of every fiscal year. The higher up you go, the more you'll make and the hotter it gets. But you will be part of the organization's decision-making inner sanctum, and almost irreplaceable if you are any good at all. (Salary information for the various types of development work is published each year by CASE and the NSFRE. They will be happy to send you a copy.)

Among the nonfinancial benefits of development writing is the opportunity to control the pace of your work, to see jobs through from start to finish, to interact with persons at all levels of the organization, and to use creative talents on a variety of assignments. And, of course, as I mentioned earlier, fund-raising writing affords an excellent career development path through professional groups, seminars, and the high demand for competent people.

## *Exercises*

- Scan your local want ads for development jobs of all kinds.
- Go to a university or college library and scan the most recent copies of "The Journal of Higher Education" and "The Chronicle of Philanthropy" for writing jobs in your area or an area in which you would like to work. Send one or two of them your resume and a letter of inquiry.
- Work free for local nonprofit agencies who need help with their fund-raising writing and publications. (There will be many.)

- Seek paying freelance assignments from large or small non-profit development offices.
- Even if you don't see a job that interests you, go to some of the places you think you would like to work and register with the human resources or personnel office to let them know you are available. They keep standing files on professionals such as writers for future reference.
- Network like mad. Try to find a friend in development work. Someone who belongs to the NSFRE, works at a university or nonprofit agency, knows a dean or director, has a job in corporate or foundation giving, or is the mother, sister, or cousin of any of the above. Rack your brain. They say you can meet anyone in the world through just five people.
- Sit down and make a plan and a timeline for getting into the field of fund-raising writing. Put it into action.

# References

I am not telling you to read all the books and publications listed below. I don't even know if you can find some of them anymore. But they represent a handful of the many books I have found both helpful and interesting over the last thirty years or so. The list could be longer by many dozens. I just want to show the variety and quality of material available to you that impinges on a writer's life and work.

You will have sources of your own, no doubt, and some of mine are probably already familiar to you. I do hope you will read a few with the same pleasure and sense of enlightenment that I have. The organizations and publications I have listed remain the leading sources of new ideas and new information in the field of fund raising and fund-raising writing.

## Organizations

*The National Society of Fund Raising Executives*
1101 King Street, Suite 700
Alexandria, VA 22314
(703) 684-0410
FAX (703) 684-0540

*Council for Advancement and Support of Education*
Suite 400, 11 Dupont Circle
Washington, D.C. 20036
(202) 328-5900

## Publications

*CASE Currents*
*Council for Advancement and Support of Education*
Suite 400, 11 Dupont Circle
Washington, D.C. 20036
(202) 328-5900

*Chronicle of Higher Education*
1255 Twenty-third Street, NW
Washington, D.C. 20037

*Chronicle of Philanthropy*
1255 Twenty-third Street, NW
Washington, D.C. 20037

*Fund Raising Management*
224 Seventh Street
Garden City, NY 11530
(516) 746-6700 • FAX (516) 294-8141

## Books: Fund Raising

*Designs for Fund Raising*
Harold J. Seymour
Fund Raising Institute

## Books: English and Grammar

*The Chicago Manual of Style*
The University of Chicago Press

*The Elements of Style*
William Strunk, Jr. and E.B. White
Macmillan

*The Mother Tongue: English and How It Got That Way*
Bill Bryson
William Morrow & Company, Inc.

*The Story of English*
Robert McCrum, William Cran, and Robert MacNeil
Viking

*Understanding Grammar*
Paul Roberts
Harper & Row

## Books: Speeches

*The Speech Writing Guide*
James J. Welsh
John Wiley & Sons

*The Power of Eloquence*
Thomas Montalbo
Prentice-Hall

*What I Saw At The Revolution*
Peggy Noonan
Random House

# Books: Direct Mail

*Successful Direct Marketing Methods*
Bob Stone
Crain Books

*The Do-It-Yourself Direct Mail Handbook*
Murray Raphel & Ken Erdman
The Marketers Bookshelf

*On the Art of Writing Copy*
Herschel Gordon Lewis
Prentice-Hall

*Making Direct Response Fund Raising Pay Off:*
*Outstanding Fund-Raising Letters and Tips*
Jerry Huntsinger
Teach 'em Inc.

# Books: Nonprofit Management

*Managing the Non-Profit Corporation:*
Principles and Practices
Peter F. Drucker
Harper Collins

*The Effective Executive*
Peter F. Drucker
Harper & Row

*Managing in Turbulent Times*
Peter F. Drucker
Harper & Row

# Books: Creative Thinking and Planning

*Art and Reality: Ways of the Creative Process*
Joyce Cary
Harper

*The House of Intellect*
Jacques Barzun
Greenwood Publishing Group, Inc.

*The Modern Researcher*
Jacques Barzun & Henry F. Graff
Harcourt Brace Jovanovich

*Science, The Glorious Entertainment*
Jacques Barzun
Harper & Row

*Experiences in Visual Thinking*
Robert H. McKim
Brooks/Cole Publishing Company

# Books: Graphic Design and Typography

*Production for the Graphic Designer*
James Craig
Watson-Guptill Publications

*Editing by Design: A Guide to Effective Word and Picture Communications for Editors and Designers*
Jan V. White
R.R. Bowker

# Books: Writing

*On the Art of Writing Copy*
Herschel Gordon Lewis
Prentice-Hall

*Elements of the Essay*
Robert E. Scholes
Oxford University Press

*Ogilvy on Advertising*
David Ogilvy
Random House

*Writers at Work*
*The Paris Review Interviews*
Edited by George Plimpton
Penguin Books

*Writing that Works*
Kenneth Roman and Joel Raphaelson
Harper & Row

*Style*
*An Anti-Textbook*
Richard A. Lanham
Yale University Press

*The Collected Essays, Journalism and Letters of George Orwell*
Edited by Sonia Orwell and Ian Angus
Harcourt Brace Jovanovich

# Common Fund-Raising Terms

**Annual giving, annual fund**
A concerted direct mail or telephone appeal to current and former donors to provide "unrestricted" funds to meet or offset an organization's annual operating expenses. These campaigns usually focus on securing large numbers of small gifts of cash. Such appeals are made anywhere from four to twelve times a year.

**"Ask"**
The moment of truth in any fund-raising conversation, letter, or proposal. This is when you spell out for the prospect exactly what you want them to support, how much you hope they will give, and when you would like them to give it. It is the nonprofit version of "closing the deal" and should never be omitted or put off until later.

**Capital campaign**
A multiyear solicitation of "major" gifts from an organization's leading group of donors and prospects until the final campaign goal is reached. Such campaigns used to take place only about once every ten years, but may now occur every three years or so. The term "capital" refers to the fact that donors are expected to make gifts drawn from their capital reserves, not just from earnings on principal.

**Case statement**
The principal document setting forth the aims and goals of a capital campaign. Quite literally, the argument, or "case," for supporting an organization's special mission.

**Charitable giving, gifts**
Gifts made by foundations, corporations, and individuals in support of publicly supported organizations whose activities qualify for exemption from federal income taxes under section 501 (c) (3) of the Internal Revenue Code.

**Chronicle of Philanthropy**
The weekly newspaper reporting and analyzing on developments, trends, and events in the fund-raising world, including recent major gifts, legislative changes, and new IRS interpretations and requirements.

**Corporate giving, gifts**
Business support for nonprofit agencies and organizations, usually those operating among the company's employment or customer bases.

## Development

The advancement of an organization's mission by securing and cultivating a permanent base of charitable support for its aims, needs, and opportunities. Also, the professional staff that plans and carries out these activities.

## Development officer

A management-level professional fund raiser. In most large organizations, the ranking fund raiser will be a vice-president.

## Direct mail

The solicitation of gift support through written appeals to a large audience. Direct-mail campaigns are used in conjunction with telethons to increase annual giving or in behalf of specific goals, such as a new building or an important new program. Such campaigns must be highly orchestrated and meticulously planned to succeed.

## Donor, major

Usually a donor who ranks among the top ten percent of institutional supporters: one whose gifts are indispensable to the success of a campaign or goal.

## 501 (c) (3)

Usually, this refers to the letter authorized by the district director of the Internal Revenue Service certifying an organization as publicly supported and tax-exempt, thereby qualifying it to receive tax-exempt donations. Copies of this letter must be attached to all grant requests or proposals.

## Foundation, charitable

An organization whose sole purpose is the distribution of its endowment and invested funds to publicly supported agencies, such as schools, hospitals, or churches, whose aims coincide with the foundation's purposes, interests, or goals.

## Gift book, gift recognition book

A publication intended to publicly honor the organization's donors, usually by printing their names or pictures or both in conjunction with a report on the year's fund-raising activities and successes.

## Gift in kind

The awarding of services, equipment, or use of facilities to a nonprofit agency in lieu of a cash donation. Such gifts may or may not be tax-deductible, depending on the circumstances in which the gift is made.

## Gift receipt

A brief form or letter signed by a nonprofit's treasurer or chief financial officer acknowledging receipt of a donor's gift. In addition to expressing the organization's gratitude, receipts usually state the amount of the gift and the date it was received. Receipts, which should be sent out as soon as a gift comes in, thus provide the donor with a record for tax purposes and also encourage additional gifts in future.

## Grant
A gift to a nonprofit agency, usually from a foundation, made in response to an earlier proposal. Grants are made for specific amounts over a definite period of time and often have special terms and reporting requirements.

## Grant guidelines
A letter, booklet, or brochure spelling out how a foundation or corporation wishes to receive applications for support. Such guidelines, which may also be included in an organization's annual report, should be followed exactly unless permission to deviate has been granted in advance. Grant guidelines can usually be easily obtained by a letter, phone call, or Fax inquiry.

## Leadership groups
Those donors who regularly contribute large gifts to nonprofit organizations at predetermined minimum levels. Membership in such groups usually entitles donors to special distinction, including honors and awards, and invitations to lectures, dinners, or receptions. For most participants, the social or professional advantage of belonging to a leadership group more than offsets the cost.

## LYBNT ("lybunt")
An acronym used to describe donors who contributed to the annual appeal "last year, but not this year."

## Mailing lists
Names and addresses of addresses of past or potential donors. These must be updated regularly or supplemented by lists purchased from list brokers or other organizations. Companies now exist who will, for a fee, examine a nonprofit's lists and rate the giving potential of donors on the basis of such factors as addresses, credit ratings, lifestyles, age, education and so on. Mailing lists are the modern day version of panning for gold; sometimes you find it, sometimes you don't.

## Mission statement
A brief statement which sums up an organization's reasons for being. Foundations often require a copy of the mission statement when considering a nonprofit's grant application.

## Named gifts, named gift opportunities
Usually large-ticket items, these offer the donor an opportunity to link his or her name with a nonprofit's buildings, facilities, or services, including, in the case of colleges and universities, professorships, scholarships, and fellowships. Named gifts thus represent the opportunity to gain an immortality of kind in exchange for cash.

## Nonprofit agency, "nonprofit"
Any publicly funded agency, institution, or organization which has been recognized by the Internal Revenue Service with 501 (c) (3) status.

## National Society of Fund Raising Executives
The management organization which sets the standards for professional fund-raising practices and confers certification on those members who successfully pass its examinations. Once certified, members are entitled to use the initials, CFRE (certified fund-raising executive) after their names.

## Overhead recovery
A percentage over and above requested grant funds which is awarded by federal agencies and some foundations and corporations toward a nonprofit's operating expenses.

## Planned giving
A service offered by most nonprofits which encourages and helps donors to leave them bequests in their wills or allows donors to defer gifts until they or their last beneficiary have died. Some of these arrangements pay donors an annuity during their lifetime in exchange for a gift of the remaining principal. These agreements have various names, including "pooled income funds" and "charitable remainder trusts."

## Pledge card (or "response device")
That part of a mailing or personal appeal to a donor on which the donor's gift amount may be entered, endorsed by the signature of the donor, and returned to the development office for recording. Although pledge cards bear considerable emotional and ethical weight, they are in no way contractual and should never be construed as such.

## Premium
Tokens or considerations offered to donors in acknowledgment of their participation. If premiums exceed the maximum value set by the Internal Revenue Service, they must be subtracted from the amount of the gift claimed as a charitable deduction. Donors have the option of declining premiums and other considerations to claim the full value of the deduction.

## Private gift, gifts
Any gift made by an individual or nongovernmental foundation or organization in support of nonprofit activities. A gift from The Pew Charitable Trusts or IBM Corporation, for example, is a private gift. A grant from the National Institutes of Health is not.

## Proposal
Any letter, document, or oral proposition from a nonprofit agency to any funding source seeking its financial support and participation in the nonprofit organization's mission. Most written proposals follow a standard for-

mat or conform to the guidelines set forth by the funding agency or individual. Proposals may also be submitted or dispatched electronically over computer networks.

## Prospect
Any person or organization considered likely to respond favorably to a nonprofit organization's appeals for support. A potential donor.

## Special event
Any public gathering or ceremony aimed at recognizing donors or involving them more closely with a nonprofit agency's goals and activities. These range in scope from lectures, award dinners, and receptions to golf tournaments, theater nights, or alumni meetings. The idea behind special events is to combine entertainment with relatively painless communications about the nonprofit's purpose, achievements, needs, and opportunities. A special event can thus be both an introductory and a reinforcing activity.

## Stewardship
The vital function of acknowledging a donor's importance to the mission of the nonprofit organization. Stewardship begins with the first gift receipt and should extend over the lifetime of the donor. This relationship should be maintained and strengthened through a well-planned program of gift receipts, thank-you notes, special events, periodic communications through newsletters, gift books, or audiovisual productions, and renewed appeals to sustain or increase giving. Major donors may require regular stewardship reports detailing the outcome of their grants.

## Telethon
An annual, semiannual, or quarterly telephone appeal to all past and potential donors asking them to renew or a make a commitment to support a nonprofit agency. Such solicitations are usually carried out in conjunction with direct mail activity both before and after calls are made. In addition to securing direct contributions, telethons help to prune and strengthen mailing lists for future appeals. In rare cases, they can even lead to major donations. In most instances, telethons are conducted by professional telemarketers with the aid of volunteer callers sympathetic to the nonprofit organization.

## Unrestricted gifts
Unrestricted gifts are donations whose use or application is left up to the recipient by the donor. Because they may be applied at the discretion of the nonprofit organization without restriction to time or purpose, these gifts are highly prized. Annual fund gifts are the most common form of unrestricted gifts.

# Index